BREAKING THE
TAX CODE

BREAKING THE
TAX CODE

AMERICA'S LEADING TAX PROFESSIONALS REVEAL PROVEN STRATEGIES TO LEGALLY

MINIMIZE
YOUR TAXES

AND KEEP MORE OF WHAT YOU EARN

TABLE OF CONTENTS:

FOREWORD
BY NATE HAGERTY 11

CHAPTER 1
HOW TO DECREASE YOUR BUSINESS TAXES BY THOU$ANDS WITH ONE SIMPLE CHANGE
BY GINA WELLER, ABA, ATP, CEC 15

CHAPTER 2
THE AUDIT AND BEYOND: TAKING ON THE IRS
BY SALVATORE P. CANDELA, EA, ABA, ATA, RFC 27

CHAPTER 3
HEALTH CARE TAX CHANGES
BY RICHARD A. LINDSEY, CPA 39

CHAPTER 4
OWNING A BUSINESS
– THE LAST LEGAL TAX SHELTER LEFT IN AMERICA
BY DOMINIQUE MOLINA, CPA, CTC 53

CHAPTER 5
"HOW TO DEDUCT YOUR KID'S BRACES!"
HEALTH REIMBURSEMENT ARRANGEMENT – CODE SECTION 105
BY JERAMY SMITH, CPA 79

CHAPTER 6
TAX PLANNING
BY LARISA HUMPHREY 91

CHAPTER 7
BREAKING THE TAX CODE
– EAT, DRINK, BE MERRY – AND DOCUMENT,
DOCUMENT, DOCUMENT
BY GARY D. HELDT, JR., CPA 105

CHAPTER 8
TAX SHELTERS
BY JIM HENDERSON, CPA 119

CHAPTER 9
THE TAX SAVVY DIVORCE
BY GARY D. KANE, CPA, MSA 135

CHAPTER 10
**TIPS, TECHNIQUES AND LITTLE KNOWN
SECRETS OF REAL PROPERTY OWNERSHIP**
– STILL THE GREATEST "TAX SHELTER" IN THE INTERNAL
REVENUE CODE
BY JOHN E. WALTERS, MBA, EA 145

CHAPTER 11
**HOW TO STAY OUT OF TROUBLE WITH THE IRS
(AND WHAT TO DO IF YOU ALREADY ARE....)**
BY DARRIN MISH, ESQ. 157

FOREWORD

In my years of working with thousands of tax and accounting professionals across the United States and Canada, I've seen many kinds. Of course, there is the standard stereotype of the pencil-pushing numbers geek – with all of the personality of a thumbtack, and the communication skills that go along with it.

And sure, we want our tax professionals to be wonky, and we want them to be excellent at keeping up with the tax code (which is a weekly endeavor, with Congressional maneuverings being what they are).

But as a small business owner (who has fired his share of poorly-performing accountants and bookkeepers), and a father of young children, I've learned to place an emphasis on those tax accountants who not only can control the tax code like a lion tamer ... but who are pro-active about communication, consultation and **relationship.**

There are very good reasons why most tax accountants are terrible at this basic business, and life skill. Most fly through tax season, hopped-up on caffeine and navigating through a blizzard of forms, paperwork, staff concerns and client requests.

But the authors in this book have made a commitment, over the years, to set up systems within their firms which enable them to find **creative solutions for just about any kind of tax or accounting conundrum in which a family or busi-**

ness owner might find themselves.

They are all leaders who proved their worth, got good at what they do, and most importantly, are willing to share it with you. All of them came from ordinary backgrounds, but yet have created relationships (and **results**) for their clients which transcend the ordinary, and truly create financial well-being for generations.

This book is full of leaders in the accounting and tax field who've 'been there, done that' and come out on top – despite all the 'dream stealers' trying to take them down. They are survivors, many overcoming large obstacles, both physical and financial, and a few mental roadblocks as well.

The lessons in this book would take years to learn – possibly a lifetime or maybe never. Reading it is like sitting in the middle of a table in a brainstorming meeting attended by some of the best minds in tax accounting.

I'd consider you lucky to have discovered this book. Sit down in a quiet place and get to know your authors, and when you're finished, rest with the confidence that yes, the tax "code" can, in fact, be broken.

Here's to financial peace for you, your family and/or your business,

Nate Hagerty
Small Business Owner, Coach and Friend To Thousands of Tax Accountants in North America

CHAPTER I

HOW TO DECREASE YOUR BUSINESS TAXES BY THOU$ANDS WITH ONE SIMPLE CHANGE

BY GINA WELLER, ABA, ATP, CEC
OWNER, WELLER CONSULTING

Do you have an entrepreneurial spirit? Does the thought of starting your own business excite you? Do you wake up every morning grateful that "you" are the boss?

Few things in life elicit the same thrill for an entrepreneur more than knowing they can get up every day, do what they are passionate about, and actually get paid to do it! This hardly seems like work, does it?

It is so easy for that "free spirit" to get so caught up in

enjoying the dream of their business, that they sometimes don't spend much time thinking about, researching, or implementing the most important aspect of the start-up process – choosing and forming the proper legal entity with which to operate their business.

Getting proper guidance and help with this decision in the beginning is crucial, and can save you money, time, and unnecessary headaches in the long run. The key word in that last sentence is **proper** guidance, not just guidance about what your choices are.

Would it pique your interest if I told you that this one seemingly unimportant decision could be the very decision that allows you to put **THOUSANDS** more into your pocket each year in spendable cash through tax savings? I don't know about you, but I sure would rather see **THOUSANDS** more in my bank account each year than in Uncle Sam's!

What? … putting **THOUSANDS** more in your pocket each year with tax savings? Let's explore this concept deeper by comparing two local business owners and competitors. We will call them Harry* and Stan*. Harry got some great advice in the beginning stages of setting up his business from an advisor. He was advised on which entity choice was right for him and his business, and which would save him the most in taxes each year. Stan, on the other hand, decided to use the internet to explore his business entity options. He decided to go with the easiest and cheapest route without getting any further advice. He decided he would just revisit this in a few years if his business actually took off. Let's see how each is doing after two years in business.

Harry works hard as do most business owners, but he also enjoys being able to take advantage of the perks and freedoms his business allows him. His advisor educated him on his choices of entity structures he could choose from, while tying it all together with many legal business deductions and business strategies that Harry never knew existed.

Implementing the proper legal structure, deductions and strategies into his business has saved Harry a minimum of $20,000 per year in taxes, when compared to Stan. With these tax savings, Harry was able to take his entire family on a cruise to the Bahamas this summer, and came back with an awesome tan. He also just bought himself a new SUV to go with that tan and is sporting it around town now with his new business sign on the door. Harry can't wait to visit his advisor next quarter to see how much money he is going to save on his taxes this year. He is already thinking about what he is going to do with the extra money. Ahh... life is good...

*Harry and Stan are fictitious characters. Any resemblance to 'real life' clients is strictly coincidental.

Stan also works hard, but is really troubled by his tax bill, which rose significantly this past year when he went in to get his taxes done. Stan now dreads to see April 15th coming each year, because he knows he will be writing out a big check payable to the Internal Revenue Service. This year, when Stan wrote out that check, he couldn't quite remember the reason he decided to go into business in the first place.

Stan feels like no matter what he does or how hard he works, he just never can seem to get ahead. To him it seems like the more money he makes in his business, the less money he has to spend on himself. If that wasn't enough, Stan had a customer threaten to sue him the other day if he didn't take care of an issue that the customer claimed his employees caused. Stan is now wondering if he is going to be held personally liable if the customer decides to follow through with his threat to sue.

Stan is perplexed. He really can't figure out how Harry, his competitor down the street, can afford to be driving around town in that new SUV promoting his business with a smile on his face, and how in the world does he have time to take off for a vacation to get that tan? Stan can't remember the last vacation he took. He knows that Harry isn't getting any more business than he is, but there is definitely something different in the way their businesses look and operate. Stan thinks to himself ... "What am I missing?"

At first glance, it may appear that Harry is better at promoting and providing services in his business than Stan, and that is why he has more spendable cash each year from his business. While this could be one reason Harry has more money to spend each year, in this case it isn't. They both have a business with similar income and service levels, and Stan and Harry are both quite knowledgeable in their chosen trades. The reason Harry manages to end his year with more spendable cash in his business than Stan is because Harry spent the time necessary when setting up his business to get guidance on the parts of his business about which he wasn't so knowledgeable. He has a properly setup entity structure which serves him well, protects him personally, and helps him put about $20,000 more per year in spendable cash in his pocket than Stan, due to tax savings.

Fortunately for Stan and many other current business owners in Stan's position, help IS available. The original choice of entity when a business is started is not usually a decision which cannot be changed, regardless of the age of the business.

With proper guidance and advice, even Stan can turn his business around and start feeling the joy of spending or saving an additional $20,000 each year, instead of sending it to the Internal Revenue Service. Then he will again remember why he decided to go into business for himself. Having your own business can truly be the American dream. Not getting the proper advice can turn it into the American nightmare! It is this very scenario that drove me to open my practice back in 2001.

After graduating college and working for businesses both large and small as an accountant for about 7 years, I knew that at some point I wanted to be in business for myself. At that time, I just wasn't sure how that was all going to evolve. Well, as luck would have it, I seemed to be at the right place at the right time and had the opportunity to learn a new skill. That skill, coupled with my current accounting knowledge, would allow me to branch out after a year on my own as a freelance business consultant. I specialized in software implementation in the area of finance and tax for large businesses.

What I found out really quickly was that I was now a 1099 contractor instead of a W2 employee as I always had been, and the tax issue became a huge part of my life that first year.

Signs of the American nightmare had started for me.

When my tax liability approached an astounding high five figures that first year, I knew that there had to be something more I could do to control this. What I remember seeing when I started reading tax articles were headlines such as "secrets of the rich", or "secrets the IRS doesn't want you know about." This convinced me that I must be missing a piece to this puzzle, so I spent the better part of the next 7 years studying anything and everything I could possibly get my hands on that would help save on my taxes – including Internal Revenue Service Publications and Code.

Through my studies, it lead me to change my businesses legal structure, use multiple entity strategies at times to shift income to lower tax brackets, and start to use a host of other deductions and loopholes the Internal Revenue Service had created yet most tax advisors were not talking about. It all became somewhat of a game to me to see how much income I could earn, and how low I could legally drop my tax bracket each year. I became very excited about all that I was learning and would often share my newest-found strategy with anyone who would listen.

In 2001, I decided to open up a practice where I could spend my time focused on helping both individuals and business owners save as much on their taxes as legally possible. This has been and still remains my passion in life today.

I love to speak with people who are thinking of opening a business and hear the passion in their voice about what it is they want to do in their new business – and be able to know that I can help them fulfill that dream with the best advice possible on the entity structure, tax strategies and liability protection they can put into place.

Working with current business owners, and showing them how to put more money in their pockets through the appropriate legal entity, as well as by using tax strategies they had no idea existed, is just as rewarding to me as it is to the business owner.

Following is a list of the types of the most common business entities available, along with some brief information about each type. It is by no means meant to be an all-inclusive list, and should not be used as the only information from which you use to decide which entity is best for you.

- Sole Proprietorship – an unincorporated form of business with one owner. It is not a separate legal entity from its owner and provides very little, if any, liability protection to the owner. For tax purposes, all income and expense of the business are reported on the personal return of the owner on a Schedule C. In addition to income taxes due on the net profit of the business, the sole proprietor is also subject to self-employment taxes (Social Security & Medicare) which is currently at 15.3%.

- Partnerships – there are two types of partnerships. General and Limited. A General partnership does not require any formal registration with a state, while the Limited partnership requires the filing of a certificate in the state in which you choose to operate. Partnerships are legal entities separate from their owners, and may or may not provide liability protection for the owners – depending on whether the owner is a general or limited partner. For tax purposes, partnerships do not pay taxes, and net income passes through to the partners personal returns. Taxes are paid by each partner on their share of income at their current tax rate. Partners may or may not be subject to self-employment taxes depending upon each partner's situation.

- Corporations – are separate legal entities from the owners or shareholders, and require registration in the state in which you choose to operate. They provide the shareholders with liability protection. For tax purposes, there are two taxation types for corporations. They can be taxed as a 'C' Corporation or an 'S' Corporation. A 'C' Corporation pays taxes at the business level and then money is distributed to the shareholders and may be taxed again at the shareholder level. An 'S' Corporation does not pay taxes at the business level, but passes the net income of the corporation to the shareholders personal return, and taxes are paid by each shareholder on their share of income at their current tax rate.

- Limited Liability Company (LLC) – is a legal entity separate from the members and requires registration in the state in which you choose to operate. They provide the members with liability protection. For tax purposes, an LLC can be taxed as a sole proprietor for single member LLCs, as a partnership for LLCs with two or more members, or as an 'S' or 'C' Corporation.

While there are a relatively small number of entity types from which you can choose, the legal details underlying each type can be inherently complex. It is always best to seek advice from a knowledgeable tax advisor who can look at your overall situation to help you determine which entity is best for you. The small investment you would have to make to hire a competent advisor could save you thousands in the future.

There are three major variables which a wise business advisor should use to help you determine which option is right for you. These variables are business control, owner liability and tax implication. If an advisor is not able to discuss all three variables with you in your decision process, then find another advisor!

As a purchaser of this book, I know that you are committed to finding out as much as you can about how to keep more money in your pocket through tax savings. If you are a current business owner or if you are thinking of starting a business, I am offering to you a special **FREE** gift which you can claim at www.wellerconsulting.com/taxcodeoffer.php. This URL is only available to owners and readers of this book.

I know that I am truly blessed to be able to share my passion and knowledge every day with those who need and want my help. It is an awesome feeling to know that I can touch so many lives and make them better – with the knowledge I will pass along.

I look forward to meeting each and every one of you who

are ready to move your business to the next level, or those of you who have a business dream in your heart.

For more information or to schedule a consultation, please feel free to visit my website at: www.wellerconsulting.com, email me at: gina@wellerconsulting.com or call my office at 888-327-9306.

Don't forget to claim your **FREE** gift at: www.wellerconsulting.com/taxcodeoffer.php.

ABOUT GINA

Gina Weller is the Owner of Weller Consulting, a tax, accounting and business consulting firm which offers "outside the box" solutions for their clients.

Gina has over 22 years of experience in a wide range of business environments. She has worked with both big and small businesses as well as public and private.

She has built her business around the principle of educating and helping others. Her diverse knowledge and experience allows her to bring new and innovative ideas to her clients.

When you bring Gina onto your team, you can feel confident that you are partnering with a professional who is honest and reliable and who will always have your best interest in mind.

Gina lives in Alpharetta, Georgia with her husband James, their son Garrett, and Missy their yellow lab.

You can contact Gina by phone at: 888-327-9306 or by email at: gina@wellerconsulting.com.

CHAPTER 2

THE AUDIT AND BEYOND: TAKING ON THE IRS

BY SALVATORE P. CANDELA EA, ABA, ATA, RFC
THE TAXADVOCATE GROUP

*"America is a land of taxation that was
founded to avoid taxation."*
~ Laurence J. Peter

When you do something on your tax return that's obviously not kosher and an IRS audit flags it, there's not a whole lot you can do about it. Taking a deduction that's not allowed, hiding income that plainly *is* income or doing anything else that's blatantly against IRS rules means you have to pay the price if you're caught. Lying about it can only get you into more trouble (just so you know – people go to jail in this country for lying to federal agents, which is what an IRS revenue agent is, *not* for failing to pay their taxes).

But what happens when the IRS fights you about a tax issue that you believe is *right*? Or that, at least, is a gray issue?

That's usually when someone comes to me. I'm an Enrolled Agent. If you don't know what that is, you're no different than most Americans. If you're ever in a position where you have a tax problem with the IRS, however, you should know what an EA is. An EA can be your best friend – and your best weapon in fighting your cause.

In this chapter, I'll give you a broad overview of what your options are when the IRS does come after you for money you don't believe you owe – and what the best strategies are that will enable you to walk away with either a radically reduced tax bill – or, best of all, no tax bill at all.

The main reason I became an EA? Well, what started it all was the fact that I hated my father's accountant. I'll explain that a little later, but first, you should understand what an EA is.

THE ROLE OF AN ENROLLED AGENT

An Enrolled Agent is someone legally authorized and recognized by the IRS to represent a taxpayer at an audit or an audit appeal. Because they have a federal license instead of a state license, unlike a CPA or a lawyer, they can represent anyone anywhere in the country in an IRS dispute.

Also unlike a CPA or a lawyer, an EA only earns that designation because of his or her extensive knowledge of the federal tax code. There are only two ways to become an EA – either you work for the IRS for at least five years in a capacity in which you have to interpret the tax code on a regular basis, or you must take a very demanding two-day exam.

How demanding is it? Well, first of all, less than a third of those who take the exam pass it. Second of all - you're not allowed to use a calculator! Have you ever tried to calculate depreciation without a calculator? Don't. You'll hurt yourself.

Why would you want an EA instead of the person who prepared your tax return to represent you at an audit? Well, if that person is not a CPA or an attorney, they *are not allowed* to represent you to the IRS. They can go along to the audit and explain what they did on your tax return – but they are not allowed to argue on your behalf.

And, to be frank, you may not *want* them to argue on your behalf, even if they are a CPA. CPAs, contrary to most people's beliefs, are generally not tax experts – they are accounting experts, licensed by whatever state they practice in to help with accounting problems. When they studied to become CPAs, they primarily learned GAAP – Generally Accepted Accounting Practices – and took a little tax coursework. They don't necessarily know all the nuances of the IRS regulations.

Enrolled Agents, however, are certified by the Department of Treasury as experts on tax code. The IRS doesn't care about GAAP when they pursue an audit – they want to know how the tax laws back up what's on a return. It's more of a legal battle than a numbers game – that's why being an EA is as close to practicing law as someone without a law license can do as a profession.

And it's also why an EA can do you the most good when you do have an IRS dispute you need to resolve. An EA can go toe-to-toe with the government on the most complex tax issues, because an EA knows as much as *they* do – or possibly even more in some cases.

THE MAKING OF AN EA

So how did I come to be an EA? I said earlier it was because I hated my father's accountant – which is only partially true. My father's accountant was actually the motivating force that caused me to begin my tax education.

Like many young people just going out into the workforce, when it came time to get my taxes done, I went to the person my father used. In that accountant's eyes, I was a 'pain in the neck'. I asked a lot of questions, questions he said he didn't have time to answer.

So I decided I was going to find out those answers for myself.

I began taking accounting classes on my own, just so I'd be able to do my own taxes. And it fascinated me. Maybe I'm weird, but I started educating myself more and more on the tax code, reading books and taking more classes.

Then I started to put all that education to work outside of my own returns – I began doing returns for friends and family members at no charge, just because, believe it or not, it was a pleasurable hobby. I found it a satisfying challenge to do these returns and test my knowledge. And when I didn't know something, I made sure to find out more about it. I took more and more classes, did more and more returns, until finally I felt ready to open a little office with a bare-bones staff to do returns professionally.

As I continued on my way with my new tax business, I began to hear more and more about "EA's" – and started to research just what those two letters were all about. I found out that an Enrolled Agent was an IRS-certified taxpayer representative who had to be an expert on tax code. That was right in my wheelhouse. I took the summer off and studied for that backbreaking exam I discussed earlier in this chapter – and I passed my first time around.

Terrific, I was an official EA. But, much like a lawyer who graduates from law school, I may have known everything about the tax code, but I had no idea how to actually do anything for a taxpayer. I didn't know how to prepare a protest, put together an Offer in Compromise or deal with anything more advanced than routine IRS paperwork.

That meant three more years of education through the National Tax Practice Institute (NTPI), and finally, in the year 2000, I became an NTPI Fellow, which meant I was prepared to offer my clients' the finest representation skills available before the IRS.

Since then our business, The TaxAdvocate Group, has continued to grow and we now have three offices, two in New York (in Queens and Manhattan) and one in Fort Lauderdale, Florida. I usually have anywhere from 20 to 30 active audit cases at a time that I work on.

I'm proud to say that I aggressively represent my clients if I think they have a legitimate case against the IRS. I don't back down and I will argue up and down (and sometimes sideways if necessary!) to fight for my clients' interests.

THE AUDIT

The first sign of trouble with the IRS is when you're notified of being audited. If you ever get an audit letter, the number one thing I would advise you (whether you hire me or not) is *don't ever represent yourself* with the IRS.

Why? Because the IRS agent serving as the auditor represents the government, not you. He or she does not have your interests at heart. You need someone to advocate your position – and it shouldn't be you. It should be someone who understands the tax code and can argue knowledgably on your behalf.

As a matter of fact, I even advise the taxpayer not to go to his or her own audit. You will get too personally involved and that could come back to haunt you.

For example, when IRS agents ask me a question about my client's return, I give as short an answer as possible. They like to just stare at me to see if I'll say anything more – to be more accurate, to see if I'll say too much and reveal something I shouldn't. Silence is one of their chief weapons – because a taxpayer, not knowing how they work, will continue talking until they either end up contradicting themselves or say something that the IRS agent will pounce on.

An expert representative, however, will only say enough to answer the question. We know when to keep our mouths shut.

The other thing is that you never know what kind of mindset the auditor will have. Some come in 100% against the taxpayer's position, no matter what. These people you don't even bother arguing with – better to wait and appeal the audit (which, to be honest, is what you really ultimately want anyway) instead. Some will be tough but fair. But the main thing to remember is that the auditor is there to push the government agenda. He or she is not there to 'make nice' with you or bend over backwards to accommodate a questionable deduction. They are there because a mistake has been flagged and they want you to pay for that mistake.

And that's why an audit is the *worst* place to attempt to negotiate a settlement.

If you think you're right but the auditor will not budge, then you have the right to speak to the group manager of the auditor's team. Most of the time, however, the group manager won't do anything to overrule the auditor's initial decision – but it's still important to speak to the group manager, however, in order to establish your first step to disagreeing with the audit outcome.

THE AUDIT APPEAL

You might think that filing an audit appeal is a useless step. You're still arguing with the IRS, which is the agency that made the initial decision against you in the audit, right?

Yes, that's true. But the audit appeal process is designed to *encourage* a settlement if the taxpayer has a legitimate case.

Let's take a few steps back and explain how the appeal process works. You'll receive the Reviewing Agent's Report (the RAR) after your audit is over. With that report comes the IRS form that you can fill out to file an appeal to your audit. If the amount in question is less than $25,000 for a tax year, you can do an informal appeal (the overall total can be more than that – for instance, the IRS may say you owe $40,000, but if $17,000 is from one tax year and $23,000 is from another, you can still do an informal appeal). If it's more than $25,000 for a single tax year, you can file a formal appeal.

In either case, you have 30 days to file that appeal – which is exactly what you *should* do. Because, again, you have a much better chance at a beneficial settlement if you move forward to an appeal.

That's because appeal officers are 'a completely different animal' to the auditors. Their goal is to work out differences. Again, if something is just plain 'black and white' wrong, you won't get any further with an audit appeal. But if it is something that's open to interpretation – and with 80,000 pages in the tax code, there is a LOT open to interpretation – the appeals process could very well work in your favor.

Why? Basically the IRS doesn't want a case to drag on too long. More importantly, it doesn't want most cases to go to the next step – tax court.

Auditors aren't allowed to consider the implications of a taxpayer case advancing to tax court – the appeal officer must. They have to think about the consequences of the government losing a case in tax court – and possibly upending part of the tax code as it applies to *all* taxpayers, which could ultimately cost the IRS a lot of money. So they research an appeal and look at the law and figure out what their chances of winning in tax court might be.

That means if they think they could lose, your appeal will probably "win."

TAX COURT

Let's say your appeal outcome isn't to your satisfaction. The IRS then gives you 90 days to file a case with the United States Tax Court. The Tax Court was established by the U.S. Constitution and has 19 presidentially-appointed members.

An EA is not allowed to represent you to the Tax Court unless they pass an even more rigorous exam – an exam that has a passing rate of only 3 or 4%. This is one river I can't take the time to cross, as I would probably have to take a year off to study for it. One colleague of mine failed this exam the first time – and the second time, when they sent him his results, he was so nervous it took him two days before he could bring himself to open the envelope!

You can only present your case to the Tax Court once (although in some cases you can appeal). But, much like the audit appeals process, the mindset here is to work things out. That's why 98% of all cases never go to trial at the Tax Court – the government wants to settle these cases and make them go away.

In conclusion, I'd like to talk about one of my most interesting cases to demonstrate how a simple case where all the facts are in a taxpayer's favor can still make an audit appeal necessary.

My client was one of the original investors in *Vitaminwater*; he put in $30,000 to help launch the brand. In 2007, the Coca-Cola Company bought out the company and my client's share of the sale was 3.5 million dollars. So far, so good. Okay, more than good – incredibly amazing.

Coke agreed to pay my client 90% of the amount in 2007 – and the remaining 10% over 2008 and 2009. The problem was that the 1099 Coke sent to my client in 2007 had the entire amount on it. In other words, in the IRS' eyes, my client received $350,000 in 2007 that, in reality, he never did. The IRS kept insisting he owed taxes on the money anyway.

We ended up filing a 44 page audit appeal that ultimately saved my client $116,000 in taxes for 2007 – but it wouldn't have happened unless we *did* file that appeal.

When you're right, it's worth the fight. Again, the audit is not where you can usually win that fight – the appeal is. When you have the right representative going to the mat for you, you can take on the IRS and prevail.

I do it every day.

ABOUT SALVATORE

Salvatore P. Candela, EA has been preparing taxes since 1986, passed the EA exam in 1997, became an Enrolled Agent in 1998, and a Fellow of NTPI (National Tax Practice Institute) in 2000, and has been a featured speaker around the country.

He has earned the following credentials from the Accreditation Council for Accountancy and Taxation – Accredited Business Accountant (ABA), and Accredited Tax Advisor (ATA). He has also earned the credential of Registered Financial Consultant (RFC) from the International Association of Registered Financial Consultants.

He is the owner and founder of The TaxAdvocate Group which is focused on tax controversy resolution – with offices in New York (Queens & Wall Street), Florida, and Michigan. His firm aggressively represents taxpayers before all administrative levels of the IRS, and is committed to helping taxpayers resolve their IRS problems – *ONCE AND FOR ALL!*

Salvatore is a member of the National Association of Enrolled Agents (NAEA), the New York State Society of Enrolled Agents (NYSSEA), the National Society of Accountants (NSA), and the National Association of Tax Professionals (NATP). These memberships help him stay current with the constantly changing tax laws and enable him to protect taxpayer's rights.

CHAPTER 3

HEALTH CARE TAX CHANGES

BY RICHARD A. LINDSEY, CPA

In March 2010, two pieces of legislation, the Patient Protection and Affordable Care Act and the Health Care and Education Reconciliation Act of 2010 were signed into law. Together these pieces of legislation make the most significant reform to health care in the United States since the enactment of Medicare under the Johnson administration in 1965.

You may think health care reform is something new, but attempts to reform health care are not limited to the Johnson, Clinton and Obama administrations. Look back a century and you'll see that President Theodore Roosevelt ran for the presidency on a platform supporting national health insurance. It was included in the original Social Security Act.

BREAKING THE TAX CODE

President Richard Nixon and Ted Kennedy almost reached an agreement on health care reform, but were derailed by Nixon's early departure from office.

It may not be a new idea, but Obama and the Congress have placed a huge administrative burden on small businesses.

Health Care Reform may already have you confused, but it's not your fault. The massive health care reform bills were intentionally designed so that it was impossible for any one person to comprehend. We know those in Congress didn't even read it. They admitted it!

How can you be expected to understand it if no one has explained it to you? So, take a deep breath and relax, we're about to take aim at this confusion and make (at least some) things as clear as possible. In this chapter, we're going to focus on the tax changes that affect small businesses.

Starting in 2010, government subsidies became available for small businesses to provide employees health insurance coverage. However, the law does not require any business to purchase insurance for its employees. That said, incentives for small businesses to provide their employees with group health insurance coverage are noteworthy.

Businesses with 10 or fewer full-time-equivalent employees (FTEs) earning less than $25,000 a year, on average, are eligible for a tax credit of 35% of qualifying employee health insurance premium costs. Companies with between 11 and 25 workers and an average wage up to $50,000 are eligible for partial credits. Beginning in 2014, the small business tax credits will cover 50% of premiums through 2016.

Except in the case of a tax-exempt employer, the credit applies only to income taxes. Normally an unused general business credit can be carried back (by a small business) 5 years and forward 20 years. However, an unused credit amount cannot be carried back to a year before the effective date of the credit, so any unused credit amount for 2010 can only be carried forward.

The number of FTEs is determined by including not only the hours employees are paid for working, but also paid vacation, illness, holiday, or other paid-leave time. The employer may calculate the total number of hours of service for determining the number of FTEs by either determining the actual number of hours for which payment has been made, or by using days-worked or weeks-worked equivalents, claiming credit for eight hours for any day or 40 hours for any week in which an employee would be credited for at least one hour of work.

In calculating the credit, the employer can only include premiums which the employer paid and incurred an expense. Amounts withheld from employees are not counted, including those withheld under a Sec. 125 cafeteria plan.

> ***Example.*** *If Wonder Wags pays 80% of the premiums for employee's coverage (with employees paying the other 20%), only the 80% premium amount paid by Wonder Wags counts in calculating the credit.*

In addition, the amount of an employer's premium payments that counts when calculating the credit, may not exceed the average premium for the small group market in the particular state (or an area within a state) in which the employer offers coverage for the same arrangement. The average premium for the small group market in a state (or area) will be determined by the Department of Health and Human Services (HHS). The IRS has published this information online at www.irs.gov.

The number of an employer's FTEs is determined by dividing (a) the total hours for which the employer pays wages to employees during the year (but not more than 2,080 hours for any employee), by (b) 2,080. The result, if not a whole number, is then rounded down to the next lowest whole number.

> **Example.** For the 2010 tax year, Cycle Hut pays 5 employees for 2,080 hours of service each, 3 employees for 1,040 hours of service each, and 1 employee for 2,300 hours of service.
>
> The number of Cycle Hut's FTEs would be calculated as follows:
>
> 1. Total hours not exceeding 2,080 per employee is the sum of
>
>   10,400 hours for the 5 employees paid for 2,080 hours each (5 x 2,080)
>   + 3,120 hours for the 3 employees paid for 1,040 hours each (3 x 1,040)
>   + 2,080 hours for the 1 employee paid for 2,300 hours (maximum of 2,080)
>   _____
>
>   15,600 TOTAL hours

2. *So, the FTEs = 7 (15,600 divided by 2,080 = 7.5, rounded down to the next lowest whole number)*

The tax credit is phased out as firm size and average wage increases.

Presuming the number of an employer's FTEs exceeds 10, or if the average annual wages exceed $25,000, the amount of the credit is proportionally reduced. If the number of FTEs exceeds 10, the reduction would be calculated by multiplying the otherwise applicable credit amount by a fraction, the numerator of which is the number of FTEs in excess of 10 and the denominator of which is 15. Full phase-out occurs with 25 FTEs.

Leased employees are included in the count.

The amount of average annual wages is determined by first dividing (a) the total wages paid by the employer to employees during the employer's tax year, by (b) the number of the employer's FTEs for the year. The result is then rounded down to the nearest $1,000. For this purpose, wages means wages as defined for FICA purposes (without regard to the wage base limitation).

> **Example.** *In the 2010 tax year, Candy's Cakes pays $224,000 in wages and has 10 FTEs.*
>
> *Candy's Cakes average annual wages would be $22,000 ($224,000 divided by 10 = $22,400, rounded down to the nearest $1,000).*

Assuming an employer's average annual wages exceed $25,000, the reduction is determined by multiplying the otherwise applicable credit amount by a fraction, the numerator of which is the amount by which the average annual wages exceed $25,000 and the denominator of which is $25,000. Full phase-out occurs when average annual wages reach $50,000.

For an employer with both more than 10 FTEs and average annual wages exceeding $25,000, the reduction is the sum of the amount of the two reductions. This sum may reduce the credit to zero for some employers with fewer than 25 FTEs and an average annual wage less than $50,000.

> *Example.* For the 2010 tax year, presume that Cleaning Diva, a qualified employer, has 12 FTEs earning average annual wages of $30,000. Cleaning Diva pays $96,000 in health care premiums for those employees (which does not exceed the average premium for the small group market in the employer's state).
>
> The credit is calculated as follows:
>
> 1. Initial amount of credit determined before any reduction: (35% x $96,000) = $33,600
>
> 2. Credit reduction for FTEs in excess of 10: ($33,600 x 2/15) = $4,480
>
> 3. Credit reduction for average annual wages in excess of $25,000: ($33,600 x $5,000/$25,000) = $6,720
>
> 4. Total credit reduction: ($4,480 + $6,720) = $11,200

5. Total 2010 tax credit: ($33,600 – $11,200) = $22,400

In calculating the employer's deduction for health insurance premiums, the amount of premiums that can be deducted is reduced by the amount of the credit.

The credit is available for regular health insurance premiums and add-on dental and vision coverage. Employers can still qualify for the credit if they receive state health care tax credits.

Seasonal workers are disregarded in determining FTEs and average annual wages unless the seasonal worker works for the employer on more than 120 days during the taxable year, although premiums paid on their behalf may be counted in determining the amount of the credit.

A sole proprietor, a partner in a partnership, a shareholder owning more than two percent of an S corporation, and any owner of more than five percent of other businesses are not considered employees for the purposes of the credit. Therefore, the wages or hours of these business owners and partners are not counted in determining either the number of FTEs or the amount of the average annual wages, and the premiums paid on their behalf are not counted in determining the amount of the credit.

Further, under the family attribution rules, a family member of any of the business owners or partners is also not considered an employee for purposes of the credit. For this purpose, a family member is defined as a child (or descendant of a child); a sibling or step-sibling; a parent (or ancestor of a parent); a step-parent; a niece or nephew; an aunt or uncle; or a son-in-law, daughter-in-law, father-in-law, mother-in-law, brother-in-law or sister-in-law. Note who's missing from the list: *a spouse*.

For 2012, businesses will be required to include the value of health care benefits they provide to employees on W-2s, beginning with W-2s for 2011. The W-2s going out in 2012 will reflect coverage provided in 2011.

While it is expected that most 2011 W-2s will be issued in January 2012, Form W-2s reflecting the new health insurance information must be available no later than February 1, 2011, in the event a terminating employee requests one. This is because employees are entitled to request their Form W-2s early if they terminate employment during the year.

Plans for which coverage costs must be reported include medical, prescription, executive physicals, Medicare supplemental policies, and employee assistance programs. Coverages under dental and vision plans must also be included unless they are "standalone" plans.

Continuing health-care insurance under COBRA must also be considered in reporting the value of employee's health care costs on their W-2 forms for 2011.

However, the cost of coverage under health flexible spending accounts, health savings accounts, and specific disease or hospital/fixed indemnity plans is excluded from the reporting.

Hidden deep inside the massive 2,409 page health care reform bill are a few lines which will unleash a flurry of paperwork on unsuspecting businesses. The new law makes key changes in 1099 requirements. First, it expands the scope from only services to include all tangible goods and second, it requires that 1099s be issued not just to individuals but also to corporations.

Beginning in 2012 companies will have to issue 1099 forms not just to contract workers but to any individual or corporation from which they buy more than $600 in goods or services in a tax year.

Businesses will have to issue billions of new tax documents each year.

Under the new rules if you buy a new computer from Best Buy, you'll have to send them a 1099. A laundromat that buys soap each week from a local distributor will have to send the supplier a 1099 at year end. The local restauranteur will have to send 1099s to each of his food suppliers, linen or laundry service, beer and liquor distributors, electrical utility, and on and on.

Payments to tax-exempt organizations should continue to be exempt from information reporting under the new law. Debit or credit card payments will also be exempt from the reporting requirements since these transactions will already be covered by reporting requirements on payment card processors.

"It's a pretty heavy administrative burden," particularly for small businesses without an in-house accounting staff according to the National Federation of Independent Businesses.

The IRS estimates that more than $300 billion is lost in unreported tax revenue each year. Using 1099s to document millions of transactions that now go untracked is one way they believe they can close the tax gap.

While the notion of mailing a tax form to Office Depot or Sam's Club each year likely seems absurd to most small business owners, it gets worse. The biggest headache will be gathering and inputting the names, addresses and taxpayer ID numbers for every vendor you do business with.

Increased record keeping could weigh heavily on small businesses. At a minimum, a significant amount of time and training is going to be required to gather, sort and input the data needed for every vendor. Even the smallest of businesses will require software to help them maintain good records.

Ignoring the requirements could lead to disaster. Businesses which fail to file information returns or file incomplete returns could be subject to a $50 penalty for each required return. For an intentional disregard of the requirement, the penalty could increase to $100 per return or more.

It might be helpful to think of the new reporting requirements as similar to payroll. In a sense, America is going on a payroll style reporting system beginning in 2012.

High-income taxpayers will be hit with two big tax hikes:

a tax increase on wages and a new tax on investments.

The new law imposes an additional 0.9% Medicare tax on wages above $200,000 for individuals and $250,000 for married couples filing jointly. In addition, for higher-income households, the new law adds a 3.8% tax on net investment income.

Currently, all wages are subject to a 2.9% Medicare tax. Workers and employers pay 1.45% each. Self-employed people pay both halves of the tax (but are allowed to deduct half of this amount for income tax purposes).

Under the provisions of the new law, which take effect in 2013, most taxpayers will continue to pay the 1.45% Medicare tax, but single people earning more than $200,000 and married couples earning more than $250,000 will be taxed an additional 0.9% (2.35% in total) on the excess over those base amounts. Self-employed persons will pay 3.8% on earnings over those thresholds.

It should be noted that the $200,000/$250,000 thresholds aren't indexed for inflation, so it is likely that more and more people will be subject to the higher tax in coming years.

Beginning in 2013, a Medicare tax will, for the first time, be applied to investment income. A new 3.8% tax will be imposed on net investment income of single taxpayers with adjusted gross income above $200,000 and joint filers over $250,000 (unindexed).

Net investment income is interest, dividends, royalties, rents, gross income from a trade or business involving passive activities, and net gain from disposition of property (other than property held in a trade or business). Net investment income is reduced by the deductions that are allocable to that income. However, the new tax won't apply to income in tax-deferred retirement accounts such as 401(k) plans.

ABOUT RICHARD

Richard A. Lindsey, CPA, also known as the "Renegade CPA," is a small business tax expert, consultant, speaker and author who helps companies and their owners keep the money they've earned instead of handing it over to Uncle Sam. He has 19 years experience as a CPA and 15 years of "in-the-trenches" work before that in the family business.

While working in the family business, Richard returned to the University of South Alabama in 1989 to earn his Master of Accounting (MAcc) degree. Upon graduation, he joined the University as an adjunct professor of accounting and a local accounting firm as a staff accountant. Richard became a partner in Zevac & Lindsey in 2000.

With Richard you get someone who understands the concerns of small business owners, someone who is focused on taxes and how they affect your business, and someone who will explain what you need to know and what you need to do about it in plain English.

To learn more about Richard, the Renegade CPA, and how you can receive free special reports and invaluable tax tips without having to wade through all the boring rhetoric and tax mumbo-jumbo, visit: www.TaxSaverTips.com or send an email to: ZevacLindsey@comcast.net.

CHAPTER 4

OWNING A BUSINESS

– THE LAST LEGAL TAX SHELTER LEFT IN AMERICA

BY DOMINIQUE MOLINA, CPA, CTC

THE TAX SHELTER CONCEPT

"Tax shelters" have been taboo ever since the modern national income tax was established in 1913. Desperate to find relief from paying "their fair share," devious taxpayers began looking for ways to escape the tax code. The names and faces have changed over the years, but the creators of these schemes abuse the boundaries of the tax law, manipulating many unsuspecting victims who are lured into the idea of reducing their greatest expense. It has become such a huge epidemic that the Senate estimates that so-called tax shelters cost the US government over one hundred billion dollars a year in lost tax revenues. The IRS even has a special unit whose sole purpose is to eliminate the countless numbers of tax shelters, attacking the logic used in their creation, and using the court system to render financial punishments to anyone daring to participate in these schemes. For this reason, I hesitate to use the term "tax shelter" to describe the amazing tax benefits available to business owners. Yet there are just no other words, which convey the power of being "sheltered" from the burdens of an expensive tax bill. Therefore, I'm including in this chapter title the terminology "...last *legal* tax shelter". You will learn, when applied correctly, a business using a solid tax plan will legally help you shelter your income well within the bounds of the law. The best part is, you will be able to sleep at night knowing that you've done everything possible to reduce your risk of an audit, and more importantly, eliminate any negative risk in an audit.

CONCEPTS TO INCREASING YOUR WEALTH

There are two basic concepts in aspiring to make more money. First, you can seek to earn more. Yet this presents a challenge as most Americans *are* seeking to earn more, yet most rarely do so (aside from annual cost of living increases). This is an especially challenging pursuit now, in these difficult economic times. The harsh reality may be that you are watching your earnings dwindle. Layoffs are rampant, and Americans find themselves doing more and making less, as employers struggle to stay afloat with pay cuts and work furloughs. Seeking to earn more is an arduous and unpredictable process. What will you do? How will you do it? When will you do it? You can *say* you'd like to earn more money, but the question is, "*can* you earn more money?" On the other hand, you can choose a defensive approach. Financial *defense* is spending less. For most Americans, taxes are our biggest expense. Therefore, it makes sense to focus your financial defense where you spend the most. Sure, you can save 15% on car insurance by switching to GEICO. But how much will that really save in the long run? Financial defense, particularly in the area of tax planning, guarantees results. You can spend all sorts of time, effort, and money promoting your business or working towards promotions at work, but that can't guarantee results.

So how do you reduce your tax and keep more of what you earn? Or even better, how can you earn more without paying tax? These questions can be answered by looking to the wisest investors and financial experts for advice.

One of the most interesting times of year comes for me when famed Billionaire, Warren Buffet, announces each tax season the percentage of tax he pays in comparison to his secretary. You may be surprised to discover that it is the humble secretary, earning just $60,000 each year in salary, who pays almost twice the tax rate of one of the world's wealthiest men.

How can this be? Is it positive proof of all the rumors that the wealthy pay very little tax while the burden of providing for our government falls on the middle class? And why does Mr. Buffet disclose this secret each year to the public?

Warren Buffet discloses this information to the public to demonstrate that owning a business and taking advantage of every available tax break is the best way to increase your wealth. Business owners have the most opportunity to create cash and wealth from an idea rather than a task. Even better, they have the most loopholes, deductions, credits, and tax breaks available for them. This combination of benefits creates the possibility of *earn*ing more and *keeping* more through tax planning.

The reason the wealthy pay less in tax is not because of how *much* money they earn. Rather it is because of *how* they earn it. It is a myth that the rich pay less in tax simply because they are rich. They pay less in tax because they have knowledge; and they can afford the right team of people to provide this knowledge. You can do what the rich do by having a plan and a method for keeping more of what you earn. Owning a business provides the method and unlocks the door to limitless ideas for reducing your tax bill.

OVERVIEW OF THE TAX SYSTEM

Let's start by taking a quick look at how the tax system works. This will "lay a foundation" for understanding the specific strategies you'll be learning about in this book.

The process starts with income. This includes most of what you'd think the IRS is interested in:

- Earned income from wages, salaries, bonuses, and commissions.
- Profits and losses from your own business.

- Interest and dividends from bank accounts, stocks, bonds, and mutual funds.
- Capital gains from property sales.
- Pensions, IRAs, and annuity income.
- Alimony and gambling winnings.
- Even illegal income is taxable. The IRS doesn't care how you make it; they just want their share! (The good news is, if you're operating an illegal business, you can deduct the same expenses as if you were running a legitimate business. If you're a bookie, you can deduct the cost of a cell phone you use to take bets.)

Once you've added up total income, it's time to start subtracting. You start with what are called, "adjustments to income." These are a group of special deductions, listed on the first page of Form 1040, that you can take whether you itemize deductions or not. Total income minus adjustments to income equals "adjusted gross income" or "AGI." Adjustments to income are also called "above the line" deductions, because you take them "above" AGI. Adjustments include IRA contributions, moving expenses, half of your self-employment tax, self-employed health insurance, Keogh and SEP contributions, alimony you pay, and student loan interest.

Once you've determined adjusted gross income, you can take a standard deduction or itemized deductions, whichever is greater. The standard deduction is $5,700** for single taxpayers, $8,400** for heads of households, $11,400** for joint filers, and $5,700** each for married couples filing separately.

Tax deductions reduce your taxable income. If you're in the 15% bracket, an extra dollar of deductions cuts your tax by 15 cents. If you're in the 35% bracket, that same extra dollar of deductions cuts your tax by 35 cents.

You can also deduct a personal exemption of $3,650** for yourself, your spouse, and any dependents.

Once you've subtracted deductions and personal exemptions, you have arrived at taxable income. At this stage of your tax return, the table of tax brackets tells you how much to pay. Its just a matter of simple math.

You may also owe self-employment tax, which replaces Social Security and Medicare for sole proprietors, partnerships, and LLCs. You'll also owe state and local income and earnings taxes.

Finally, you'll subtract any tax credits. These are dollar-for-dollar tax reductions, regardless of your tax bracket. So if you're in the 15% bracket, a dollar's worth of tax credit cuts your tax by a full dollar. If you're in the 35% bracket, an extra dollar's worth of tax credit cuts your tax by the same dollar. There's no secret to tax credits, other than knowing what's out there. It's worth mentioning at this point that many of current administration's tax proposals involve tax credits, so these will likely become an even more important part of your tax planning.

**2010 Amounts

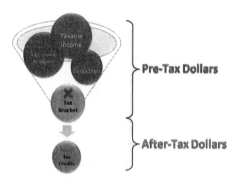

Ultimately, there are two kinds of dollars in this world: pre-tax dollars, and after-tax dollars.

Pre-tax dollars are great. And after-tax dollars aren't bad. But they're not as good as pre-tax dollars. The bottom line is:

You lose every time you spend after-tax dollars that could have been pre-tax dollars.

Subsequently, one of the key components to tax planning is the ability to shift after tax dollars into pre-tax dollars.

The problem with most middle-income taxpayers is they fall onto the endless hamster wheel of taxes and spending. They work hard, do well in school, get a good job at a stable company, pay their taxes first through paycheck withholding, and spend whatever is left over.

Employee Spending Cycle

When you are an employee, the government takes its share first; with each and every paycheck. Your ability to provide for your expenses rests in whatever amount is leftover.

On the other hand, the real key to paying a lot less in tax is learning how to shift your after tax dollars into pre-tax dollars. Owning a business provides a legal way to accomplish this. When set up correctly, a business pays its expenses first, and then pays tax on the amount leftover. By creating a business, you can control the amount of money you spend on taxes. This is how Warren Buffet and millions of other wealthy Americans pay less tax per year than an employee earning a $60,000 salary!

Business Spending Cycle

"LOOPHOLES" IS NOT A DIRTY WORD!

I speak all across the country teaching people how to use tax planning as a way to keep more of what they earn. When preparing for my media appearances, I always have to chuckle when a show producer instructs me not to use the word, "loopholes." There is a common misconception that someone using loopholes is a shady person, or someone practicing tax avoidance. The truth is that loopholes are created by the government. They <u>want</u> us to use loopholes. Loopholes are just government incentives to promote its public policy.

Most loopholes exist for business owners. More deductions, breaks, and credits exist for business owners because business is the heart of our economy. By providing breaks to businesses, our government can stimulate the economy and keep it flourishing in good times, and fuel it in recessions.

This is especially evident now, in our troubled economic times. We can clearly see Washington's stimulus geared toward businesses because small business employs people, invests in equipment and capital resources, and creates general movement of cash in our economy. In a sense, providing breaks to businesses helps to jump-start our economy. Since the government wants our economy to grow, they design the majority of stimulus aid toward business to create a change in our economic climate.

I am one of this country's top experts in the art of paying less tax, but even the very best in tax planners can only do so much for an employee paying a lot of tax. In fact, as employees earn more in their paycheck, they actually *lose* deductions, credits, and loopholes! I propose then, if you want to make more money, you must change the WAY you earn your money. It is then that you will change *how much* you make by keeping more of what you earn. This concept is financial defense at its best and will help you take charge of your financial future.

Working under this strategy of converting "post-tax" dollars to "pre-tax" dollars, you can essentially use a business to provide ways to take your ordinary spending and make it tax deductible spending. How do you accomplish this? Start a business! And I should add, start the RIGHT business.

If the idea of starting a business intrigues you, lets start by identifying the steps to create your very own (legal) tax shelter. Don't wait, you can start today!

WHAT IS A LEGITIMATE BUSINESS?

The first step to starting a business, is to start! You may

consider starting a part-time business initially as you continue to work in your full time employment. This can often be the smartest way to create tax benefits as you build your business with added tax savings as a bonus.

We are living in an age of convenience. This provides many opportunities for entrepreneurs to get started in business, in endless possibilities of activities. If you don't already have an idea for a business, evaluate your favorite activities. From a financial perspective, I recommend examining your spending habits. Where do you spend the most money? Is there a way to create a business around that activity?

I recently shared this discussion with a client, Ed, whose hobby was music. He was a faithful, devoted fan who spent most of his spare time attending concerts, meeting artists, and talking with other fans about his passion. This pursuit was clear in examining his financial records. Concert tickets, subscriptions, and music purchases were the source of much of his after tax dollars. After learning the powerful tax benefits of owning a business, the music industry was a natural option for Ed. Even without musical talent as a performer, there are many opportunities to use his expertise and skills in the area, and he went on to manage an up-and-coming rock band as a part-time business.

HOBBY LOSS RULES

Unfortunately, it is not simply the action of starting a business which enables you to take tax deductions for your after-tax dollars. Most personal time pursuits fall under what are known as the "Hobby Loss" rules, a special set of guidelines used by the IRS to eliminate your ability to deduct expenses for doing what makes you happy simply to avoid tax.

To prevent abuse of business loopholes, the IRS uses criteria to determine if, in fact, you have a hobby or a business. If you merely have a hobby, you are precluded from deducting losses related to that activity.

The beauty of incorporating a business into your tax plan however, lies in knowing the rules and structuring your business appropriately to follow the law. When you meet the IRS criteria for having a business, you can enjoy all the tax benefits that come along with your business including converting after-tax dollars into pre-tax dollars.

IRS HOBBY LOSS CRITERIA

There is no question that the IRS will gladly accept, and in fact requires your payment of tax for income generated from your business. However, the grey areas of whether or not an activity is a business or a hobby matters most when there are losses. Your ability to deduct any losses from your business will help lower your current tax bill. Meeting these criteria will enable you to deduct any losses you experience in the business against other forms of your income.

First, you must carry-on the activity in a business-like manner with a for-profit motive. This is easy to accomplish and document in case you need to defend your position during an examination. Make sure you treat your business separate from your household financial activity. This means using a separate business bank account to receive your business income and pay your business expenses. Keep organized records of your business activity. Easy-to-use bookkeeping software like QuickBooks can help organize your business financial records.

You must be involved in your activity with the purpose of making a profit. This is truly what distinguishes a hobby from a true business. I also must emphasize the importance of the word profit. It is not enough just to create *income,* but profit is what is left over after all expenses have been paid to generate your income. You should be sure and document your intention and efforts to create profit in your business. Diaries, meeting minutes, copies of advertisements and marketing plans all can support your "for profit" motive.

If you've experienced losses in your business, you should show that losses are normal for your type of business. This can be as simple as citing profit statistics for early stage businesses in your industry. Additionally, you should document your attempt to improve profitability. Again diaries, meeting minutes and marketing plans can be beneficial for proving this criteria has been met.

You should be able to prove that you, or your advisors, have the knowledge needed to carry out the activity as a business. Curriculum vitae, references from previous colleagues, and certificates from continuing education classes can help support your position. If you have had similar successful businesses in the past, be sure to include records from these experiences.

It is helpful to demonstrate that the activity has made a

profit in some years. This is not to say that if you never have a profit you are not legally entitled to deduct your losses. In fact, one recent court case featuring a farmer with 29 years of losses proved that you don't have to have a profit in order to prevail in deducting your losses. However, prior profits certainly help demonstrate the legitimacy of your activity as a business and not a hobby.

Finally, if you have a reasonable expectation of future profit, be sure and document this as well. This may be due to new marketing efforts, economic forecasts, or new revenue opportunities. Again, be sure to document these items to support your position.

CHOOSING THE RIGHT BUSINESS STRUCTURES FOR MAXIMUM TAX BENEFIT

There are 3 basic types of businesses which include **sole proprietorships** (businesses with one owner), **partnerships** (businesses with more than one owner), and **corporations** (a separate legal entity governed by state law).

Of these types, there are many different business structures.

SOLE PROPRIETORSHIPS

Most businesses start as a sole proprietorship. It is the easiest of all the entities to establish because it requires no paperwork! For this reason, it is the least expensive to operate; from an administrative standpoint that is! Sole proprietorships have certain advantages, but in general can create additional tax and audit risk. The majority of sole proprietorships I see may have been appropriate at the beginning of a business, but as the owner's needs change with time, they are no longer effective. As such, sole proprietorships, unless established for particular tax benefits, are generally not the most appropriate choice for tax planning.

If you operate your business as a sole proprietorship, you may pay as much in self-employment tax as you do in income tax. If you are taxed as a sole proprietor, you'll report your net income on Schedule C of your form 1040. In a sole proprietorship, you'll pay tax on your business profits at whatever your personal rate is. But you'll also pay self-employment tax, of 15.3% on your first $106,800** of "net self-employment income" and 2.9% of anything above that.

Sole Proprietorship Landmines
— Self-employment tax on profits, no deductibility of fringe benefits, higher risk of audit

Let's say your profit at the end of the year is $80,000. You'll pay regular tax at your regular rate, whatever that is. You'll also pay about $11,000 in self-employment tax. The self-employment tax replaces the Social Security and Medicare tax that your employer would pay and withhold if you weren't self-employed.

**2010 Amounts

Sole Proprietorship

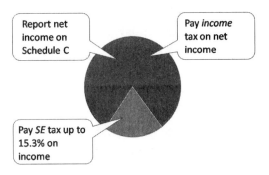

Report net income on Schedule C

Pay *income* tax on net income

Pay *SE* tax up to 15.3% on income

Sole proprietorships do not pay a separate federal income tax. As illustrated above, the profits are reported on the owner's tax return and tax is paid at the rate of the individual owner.

PARTNERSHIPS

If you have more than one person involved in the ownership of your business, you have a partnership. This is true even if you haven't formed a formal partnership agreement! Even a verbal agreement of doing business between 2 or more individuals creates a partnership.

Partnerships present some of the most complex areas of legal and tax law. As with sole proprietorships, partners in a partnership are subject to self-employment tax on the business profits. But they can be an easy way to get started in a new business without the expense of forming another type of entity.

Partnership Landmines – Self-employment tax on profits, no deductibility of fringe benefits, specialty tax issues for adding and removing partners

Partnerships are known as "pass through" entities in that the profits and losses from the partnership "pass through" to the individual owners' tax returns. In turn, the individual owners pay tax at whatever their personal tax rate. As with sole proprietorships, partnerships do not pay business federal income taxes on their profits. However, profits earned in a partnership generally are subject to self-employment tax. This sometimes can be more than the owner's federal income tax!

One convenient feature of a partnership is that partners can decide as often as they prefer how to share in profits and losses of the business. This provides great flexibility in tax planning. For example, if the business experiences losses and one particular partner can benefit from deducting the losses over another, they can simply agree to the special allocation and report these special allocations of income and deductions as they determine appropriate for the owners.

Partnership

Report net income on Schedule E

Pay *income* tax on net income

Pay *SE* tax up to 15.3% on income

S CORPORATION

A third type of business entity is the S corporation. An "S" corporation is a special corporation that's taxed like a partnership. The corporation pays you a reasonable wage for the work you do. If there's any profit left over, it passes through to you, and you pay the tax on that income on your own return. So the S corporation splits the owners income into two parts, wages and pass-through distributions.

S Corporation Landmines – Reasonable compensation audit issues, no deductibility of fringe benefits, no disproportionate distributions, loss basis issues

Here is why the S corporation is so attractive. You will pay the same 15.3% tax on your wages as you would on your self-employment income. But – there's no Social Security or self-employment tax due on the dividend pass-through. Using this tax planning strategy, S corporation owners can create tax savings through a reduction of their self-employment tax.

The S corporation, like a partnership, is a pass-through entity. Net profits are passed through to the individual shareholders, who each pay taxes on their share at their own individual rates. One restriction of the S corporation, however is that the owners cannot receive disproportionate distributions. This means that income and losses must be allocated to each shareholder according to his ownership percentage.

S-Corporation

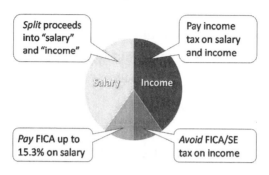

Split proceeds into "salary" and "income"

Pay income tax on salary and income

Salary

Income

Pay FICA up to 15.3% on salary

Avoid FICA/SE tax on income

CORPORATION

A corporation is a separate legal entity governed by state law. C corporations must prepare and file their own tax returns and pay tax at special corporate tax rates. Sometimes these rates can be lower than the individual owner's tax rates, providing an opportunity for tax planning to take advantage of this rate difference. The corporate tax, however, can pose an additional tax because as these profits are distributed to the shareholders in the form of dividends, the owners pay tax on the dividends at their own individual rates. I've seen many C corporations who were un-

> **Corporation Landmines** – Double tax issues, inability to "pass-through" losses to owners, specialty taxes (accumulated earnings tax, personal holding company tax, personal service corp tax issues)

necessarily paying this "double" tax on profits – first at the corporate level and then as the owners withdrew profits from the business. This is one of the major disadvantages of owning a C corporation.

C corporations have many wonderful tax benefits. They have the most deductions available of any business structure, including the ability to deduct valuable fringe benefits for the owners. C corporations are also great for growing businesses, businesses with plans to become publicly traded companies and in general, corporations with more than 100 shareholders.

C Corporation

Report net income on Corporate Tax Return 1120

Pay *income* tax on net income

Pay individual income tax on dividends

LLC

The LLC is a relatively young type of business structure which offers a hybrid between a partnership and an S corporation. It works much like a partnership or S corporation in that its profits pass-through to its individual owners. Yet unlike a partnership, the LLC contains powerful legal liability protection which can help protect its owners more than a partnership or even an S corporation.

The LLC is an extremely flexible entity structure which can be taxed many ways. For example, an LLC with a single member (1 owner) is considered a disregarded entity for federal tax purposes. For this reason, profits and losses from an LLC are reported on a taxpayer's Schedule C or Schedule E (for rental properties) of the owner's form 1040.

The LLC can also elect to be taxed as an S corporation. All the tax attributes I mentioned regarding S corporations would apply to an LLC which has elected S corporation tax treatment.

Finally, LLC's can also elect to be taxed as a C corporation. In this case, the LLC would file its own tax return, and pay taxes at corporate tax rates for its profits.

Business owners who choose to hold their business or investments inside of an LLC, generally do so to take advantage of the valuable liability protection laws governing this type of business structure. However, they can still maintain this liability protection while maximizing their tax benefits by making the proper tax elections for the entity.

LLC Landmines –
Most LLC owners make no election for how their business will be taxed. By default, an LLC is taxed either as a sole proprietorship or a partnership and receive all the disadvantages included with those entity structures.

SELECTING THE RIGHT ENTITY TO MINIMIZE YOUR TAX

You'll notice that each entity I've discussed above, has its own set of legal and tax advantages. Yet most business owners approach the decision of which business is right for them by consulting with an attorney. Their decision-making process, therefore, focuses on the legal benefits and nuances surrounding the entity choice. The side effect to approaching your business decision this way, is that you can often miss valuable tax breaks available. This happens so frequently in fact, that when I'm meeting with a new client for the first time, most have no understanding of *why* they are holding their business in a particular entity structure. And most have no idea that operating as a different entity can have monumental tax consequences.

The first thing to consider when you're trying to decide which type of business structure will work best for you, is to decide which one will be most beneficial to your tax plan. The bottom line question you should ask yourself is, "What pre-tax spending will your business structure provide you, and is this the area which will benefit you most?"

Look at your spending patterns. Where do you spend the most money? Does the business entity you are considering provide a tax advantage for this type of expense?

At the end of the day, if you're serious about getting your business to succeed, and you want to make the most of your tax plan, you're going to need some help. Nobody can be an expert at everything, and the tax code is complicated. Enlisting the help of a tax planning specialist can also provide support for the IRS Hobby Loss criteria. Make sure you work with someone who not only has good knowledge of the tax code and filing requirements, but who will work with you proactively throughout the year to make sure you are taking advantage of every available break. Do not limit yourself to working with someone face-to-face. Modern technology provides many opportunities to work with the

RIGHT advisor, even if that person is across the country, instead of across the street.

ABOUT DOMINIQUE

Dominique Molina, CPA CTC
President
American Institute of Certified Tax Coaches
CertifiedTaxCoach.com
CertifiedTaxCoach.org

Dominique Molina is the co-founder and President of the American Institute of Certified Tax Coaches. As the driving force and visionary behind the San Diego-based company, Ms. Molina set out to change the way tax professionals approach tax planning. In 2009, Ms. Molina began to create an elite network of tax professionals including CPAs, EAs, attorneys and financial service providers who are trained to help their clients proactively plan and implement tax strategies that can rescue thousands of dollars in wasted tax. Her more than 12 years of hands-on experience in the accounting and business fields provide her with ample skills to accomplish this mission. Ms. Molina has successfully licensed tax professionals as Certified Tax Coaches across the country, creating a national network of highly qualified advisors. This premier group of professionals features less than 200 specialists in 40 states who have achieved this very specialized designation.

Prior to founding Certified Tax Coach, Ms. Molina successfully managed her own practice, AccountOnIt, a San Diego-based, full-service tax, accounting, and business consulting firm, serving hundreds of business owners and investors across the country for seven years. Preceding this, Ms. Molina assisted a variety of clients for the largest independently-owned CPA firm in San Diego.

Ms. Molina received her bachelor's degree in Accounting from San Diego State University. Upon graduation, she began her accounting work as a staff accountant, controller, and office manager at several closely-held asset management and investment companies.

Ms. Molina frequently appears as a tax expert and TV guest in regional television markets. Her excellent media credentials, professionalism, and outgoing personality allow her to provide expert advice on tax issues for thousands of Americans. Ms. Molina is also a published author of two books on taxation, and has written one of our country's preeminent tax planning textbooks. A frequent lecturer and speaker, Ms. Molina often teaches at professional association conferences for tax accountants, and instructs continuing professional education courses for various organizations. Her website also receives thousands of visitors per month who follow her financial video blogs.

When not solving the challenges of America's taxpayers, Ms. Molina loves being a wife and a mother. She spends her free time with her family enjoying San Diego, surfing, tennis, reading, traveling and running. Ms. Molina is also a classical pianist.

If you're wondering if YOU pay too much in tax, visit www.CertifiedTax-Coach.com to take our free tax mistakes quiz.

CHAPTER 5

"HOW TO DEDUCT YOUR KID'S BRACES!"

HEALTH REIMBURSEMENT ARRANGEMENT – CODE SECTION 105

BY JERAMY SMITH, CPA

My clients are always asking "What all can I deduct? Can I deduct my car, phones, clothes, dry cleaning, my kid's braces, etc?" Surprising to some, the answer is more often "it depends" rather than an outright "no." How the "it depends" changes into a "yes" is largely a product of pro-active tax planning. In other words, planning and setting up your business, benefits, etc, in such a way that you can take advantage of different areas of the tax code. This chapter addresses one area of the tax code

(Code Section 105) that allows a business to deduct otherwise non-deductible health-care related expenses.

I had a client (names and medical expenses have been changed to protect the innocent!) tell me his teenager needed braces. He asked me if there was any way he could deduct those upcoming expenses. At first glance, it may seem like a completely personal expense that would be very hard to justify as a business deduction, but with proper planning, I will be able to answer the question with a resounding "YES!" Imagine his surprise when I said "Actually, yes, there is a way that your business can deduct that – from both income tax and self-employment tax!" Because of the way his business was set up and because his wife worked as the office manager taking care of daily tasks, appointment setting, travel arrangements, etc., he fit a set of circumstances that allowed him to set up a Section 105 Health Reimbursement Arrangement. (This would also work for out-of-pocket expenses for prescriptions, co-pays, deductibles, hospital stays, dental, vision, hearing, plus many others.)

A Health Reimbursement Arrangement allows a qualified business to reimburse its employees, their spouses, and their dependents for uninsured, out-of-pocket medical costs. These reimbursements are deductible by the company, but are NOT taxable to the employee.

Let me give you a brief overview of how this works. In general, your business has a W-2 employee and you wish to offer your employee this benefit. You set up the plan including the maximum amount you want to reimburse per year. The combination of the cash W-2 wages plus benefits must be reasonable compensation for the work that they do.

HOW DO I SET UP AND ADMINISTER THIS?

I personally refer my clients to a Third Party Administrator (TPA) that does most of the work to set up and maintain these plans at a very reasonable cost. I do that for three reasons:

1. In all honesty, it's probably cheaper than I could provide the same service myself, but since this is all the TPA does, and since they do it all day every day, they are able to do it more efficiently while making sure every "t" is crossed and every "i" is dotted.

2. I also prefer using the TPA since they continually stay up on the laws and make sure their plans are solid and audit-proof.

3. They have an audit guarantee and a savings guarantee.

For example, The Patient Protection and Affordable CareAct includes a catalog of comprehensive healthcare reforms that will fundamentally change the way everyone does business. In order to receive the maximum tax savings available through these plans, you will now need to adhere to a stricter set of rules and regulations. These new regulations are complex, exacting, and difficult to understand. The company I use not only makes sure the plan is compliant, but they also keep me up-to-date, so that I can help guide my clients and help them protect their tax savings.

WHAT ALL DO I NEED TO DO?

I would highly suggest you use a Third Party Administration who specializes in these plans.

Note: I had another client who wanted to set up a Health Reimbursement Arrangement, but didn't want to pay the few hundred dollars it was going to cost him, even though it was going to result in an over $4,000 tax savings in his first year. Instead, he spent hours online reading and finding documentation to try to set up the plan on his own. Had he used the Third Party Administrator I work with, he would know, absolutely, that his plan was solid and audit-proof. In fact, the TPA I use has an **"audit guarantee"** because they know, absolutely, that their plans are within the laws of the IRS.

At the time I am writing this, they also have a **"savings guarantee"**. If you do not deduct at least $2000 in a plan year, you will receive a full refund of your enrollment fee. So there really is no risk to see how much you can save.

In general, these are the items you will need to do and the TPA can help you with these:

- Have a written plan and send out Summary Plan Benefits
- Have a legitimate employee and employment contract
- Establish the compensation package
- Pay a W-2 Wage monthly or quarterly
- Reimburse Medical Expenses
- Submit benefit expenses annually to your Third Party Administrator

WHO IS THE BEST CANDIDATE FOR THIS?

In my opinion, the absolute best candidate for these plans are small family-owned businesses who can legitimately hire a spouse to take advantage of the available benefits and have enough medical expenses to make the numbers work in their favor.

But even if your business has other non-family employees, this could still be an excellent tool, as it could help you offer benefits to your employees that are non-taxable to them, and still result in a deduction for you.

Go to my website, follow the links to the company I use, and see if you qualify and find out how much you might be able to save in taxes.

DOES THIS WORK IF I AM SELF-EMPLOYED?

It can, depending on your entity type and if your spouse is an employee of yours. Let me briefly cover how this works in different types of entities, although **ALL entities** can recognize some tax savings based on their facts – so get an estimated calculation done for your company, no matter what kind of entity it is.

SOLE PROPRIETOR:

The taxpayer owns the company. He can hire his spouse to do the bookkeeping for his company and provide a compensation package that includes a W-2 wage, reimbursement of family medical insurance, and reimbursement of family out-of-pocket costs.

PARTNERSHIPS:

Let's say Mark and Craig own a business as a partnership. They can both hire their spouses and get the same treatment as the sole proprietor above.

C-CORPORATIONS:

A single person operating out of a C-Corporation can get the same benefits as the sole proprietor above. Spousal employment is NOT required in a C-Corporation.

S-CORPORATIONS:

The benefit is not as large since both the S-Corporation owner and his spouse are treated as self employed, but there is still a benefit. All benefits that go through the plan can escape the Self-employment tax. This works in a similar way to how health insurance is reported and treated for S-Corporation owners, however, only the health insurance is deducted in calculating the income tax as well. Depending on your expenses, this could still result in significant savings.

LLC:

You have to look at how the LLC files its taxes. It uses the method above based on how it files its taxes.

AM I NOT ALREADY DEDUCTING MY MEDICAL EXPENSES?

The answer is yes...and no...it just depends on all of your facts and circumstances, but the general answer is that very few people actually get much tax benefit from their medical expenses.

INSURANCE PREMIUMS

If you are self-employed, or treated as self-employed based on how your business entity is set up, you are probably deducting your health insurance premium on page 1 of your 1040, so you are saving tax at your marginal tax rate. So, $10,000 in insurance premiums would lower your taxes $2,500 if you were in the 25% marginal tax bracket.

(NOTE: For 2010 only, The Small Business Tax Act of 2010 allowed self-employed taxpayers to deduct self-employed health insurance for both Income Tax AND for self-employment tax. This currently only applies to 2010, but that is something to watch out for.)

By getting the premiums into a Health Reimbursement Arrangement, many entity types can also save Social Security and Medicare tax (another 15.3%) in addition to the marginal Income Tax rate mentioned above.

OTHER OUT-OF-POCKET COSTS

Any other allowable health care expenses are typically deducted on Schedule A – Itemized Deductions but many people never realize any true tax savings from their Schedule A. For health care expenses to make a difference on Schedule A, there are 2 hurdles to overcome.

1. You can only include the out-of-pocket costs OVER 7.5% of your adjusted gross income (that will eventually change to 10% under the new health care bill).

2. That excess is then added to your other itemized deduc- tions like Mortgage Interest, Real Estate Taxes, and Con- tributions. That total sum must then be more than your corresponding "Standard Deduction" for you to benefit by taking the Itemized deductions.

So, in reality, many out-of-pocket costs aren't deducted at all, and if they are, they are only for the Income Tax calculation and not for Social Security and Medicare tax.

SO, GET TO THE POINT... HOW MUCH CAN I SAVE???

Let's look at an example and see the potential tax savings:

Joe had a plumbing business that he operates as a sole proprietor (files Schedule C). His wife Judy works in his office part-time scheduling appointments, sending invoices, collecting payments, making deposits at bank, etc.

Joe's health insurance premiums for himself, his wife, and his 2 kids is $600/month, or $7,200 per year.

In addition, the family pays about $5,000 for out-of-pocket medical costs each year (co-pays, deductible amounts, braces, prescriptions, etc.).

Without a section 105 plan, the $12,200 Joe pays for insurance and out-of-pocket expenses would only save Joe about $1,080 in taxes.

If Joe were to restructure these expenses and implement a Section 105, Health Reimbursement Arrangement, the $12,200 Joe pays out could instead result in tax savings of around $4,270. **That's over $3,000 in real tax savings by running the same expenses through a proper Section 105 – Health Reimbursement Arrangement.**

Before having a 105 HRA plan		With a 105 HRA Plan	
Insurance Premiums	7,200	Insurance Premiums	7,200
Federal Tax Rate		Federal, State, SE taxes rate	
assume 15% marginal tax	x15%	-assume 35% tax rate (b)	x35%
Tax Savings	1,080		2,520
Out of Pocket Costs (a)	5,000	Out of Pocket Costs (a)	5,000
No deduction for these	-	Federal, State, SE taxes rate-35%	x35%
Tax Savings	-	Tax Savings	1,750
Total Expenses	12,200	Total Expenses	12,200
Total Deductions	7,200	Total Deductions	12,200
Total Tax Savings	1,080	Total Tax Savings	4,270

(a) prescriptions, co-pays, braces, etc
(b) Self employment tax =15.3%, estimated state tax = 4.7%, federal tax rate = 15%

SO WHAT SHOULD YOU DO NOW?

I would highly recommend that you go to my website for more information. From there, you can get in contact with the Third Party Administrator that I use and let them work with you to get an estimate of how much you might be able to save. From there, it is just a cost/benefit analysis. Figure out what all your costs would be to set up and admin- ister the plan, and compare that with how much you could save. My guess is that many small businesses would benefit from this plan, and the result would be extra cash in your pockets!

Visit now: www.105info.com

ABOUT JERAMY

If you're like most small business owners, you waste thousands of dollars every year in taxes you don't need to pay. Jeramy Smith wants to help you fix that.

Jeramy Smith has been a CPA in Texas since 1994. He has worked in small public accounting firms as well as in the tax department of a multi-billion dollar Dallas-based holding corporation that owned and operated businesses across a diverse range of industries.

He holds both a Bachelor's and Master's degree from Texas A&M University. He is a member of the American Institute of Certified Public Accountants, the Texas Society of Certified Public Accountants, and the National Association of Tax Professionals. He is also a QuickBooks ProAdvisor.

Education runs deep in his family. In recent years he has focused his tax work on teaching small business clients about tax saving opportunities and helping them implement real tax saving strategies.

In the summer of 2010, he started his own accounting firm, Jeramy Smith, CPA, PLLC in the north Dallas suburb of Plano. He agrees that many accountants do a fine job recording the history given to them. They compile monthly, quarterly, and annual books and records. At tax time, they put the "right" numbers in the "right" boxes in the "right" forms. But then they call it a day.

Jeramy doesn't want to just record your history; he wants to help you write it in a proactive manner. In order to minimize your taxes, you need to plan. You need concepts and strategies that leave more on your bottom line.

Mistakes and missed opportunities can cost your small business thousands in additional taxes. Jeramy will help you find those mistakes and missed opportunities and he'll provide solutions to rescue those wasted dollars.

For more information or to contact him visit: www.planotaxteam.com or email him at: jeramy@planotaxteam.com. Remember to also visit his Section 105-Health Reimbursement Website at: www.105info.com.

CHAPTER 6

TAX PLANNING

BY LARISA HUMPHREY

ARE YOU PLANNING TO FAIL?

L et me start by dispelling the common misconception that tax planning only helps multi-billion dollar companies – big business. This is just not true. In fact, it's the small business owner who benefits most from tax planning, often reducing their taxable income to $0. With proper planning, small businesses can operate tax free!

Tax planning is finding legal ways to minimize your income taxes and protect your assets. The process consists of a comprehensive review of your business and personal financial affairs, then implementing strategies to keep more money in your pocket. The plan tells you what to do to cut your tax bill as much as possible and how to do it.

This includes tactics like deducting the family's medical expenses as a business deduction, writing off your children's allowance or private school tuition and structuring your business to avoid self employment tax. The tax code is stuffed with thousands of ways to reduce your taxes, but you must have a plan.

The key to a successful tax plan is all in the preparation. You must establish each program by IRS guidelines in advance. This is not something that can be done when you file your taxes after the tax year in question is over.

You'll need an up-to-date working knowledge of the ever-changing tax laws in order to formulate strategies that will stand up to an IRS audit. I recommend you see an experienced tax professional who is proficient in tax planning and stays current on tax law changes.

In my 20 years of tax preparation, I have seen countless clients who were very excited to report they started a new business during the year and made lots of money, only to find out they owed much of their profit to the federal and state governments.

They kick, scream and fight about how unfair the tax laws are and act like Uncle Sam was punishing them for starting a business. But if you don't have a plan for income taxes, you plan to fail.

A prime example would be my clients, a married couple, let's call them the TaxSavers. They run a multi-level marketing business that has grossed around $500,000 for the past couple of years.

They learned how to operate their business effectively and became experts at recruiting new associates. They sell a great deal of the company's products and make commission not only on the products they sell, but also on the products sold by associates in their downline. The TaxSavers do a great job running their business, but failed to protect their assets and their family's future. They didn't plan for income taxes. They planned to fail.

For the past three years, the TaxSavers have owed Uncle Sam somewhere between $55,000- $75,000, depending on how well they've kept track of their expenses—which usually isn't very well. Had they kept better records, I'm sure their tax bill would have been lower. But since the TaxSavers couldn't prove many of their expenses, simply because they paid cash, didn't keep receipts or both, they were stuck with enormous tax bills each year.

Note: Please see a professional bookkeeper/accountant to have your bookkeeping done. It is well worth the cost! There is much more to bookkeeping than just data entry. In addition to keeping accurate, detailed records and providing you with reports that help you make better business decisions, a good bookkeeper is able to analyze your financial situation and give you important information that can save you a great deal of money. For instance, I had one client that didn't realize he was spending over $400 every month in ATM fees! (That's $4800 a year wasted!) Several other clients learned they could buy in bulk to save money since they were using more supplies than anticipated.

It boggles my mind how the TaxSavers continued to subject themselves to extremely high tax bills year after year, without making an effort to find a solution. Because of the way they operate their business, I knew the TaxSavers could turn many of their personal expenses into business tax deductions.

Following are the basic areas every business owner should examine when searching for tax-reducing programs. These basic strategies were sufficient for the TaxSavers because their income was only $500,000. The more income you have, the more complicated your tax plan will be.

TOP 10 TAX PLANNING AREAS

1. Entity Choice
2. Office space
3. Automobiles
4. Pay Yourself
5. Pay Your Family
6. Medical Expenses
7. Retirement Plan
8. Equipment/Furniture Rental
9. Daycare
10. Athletic Facility

1) ENTITY CHOICE: Is it costing you more?

The TaxSavers were operating their business as a sole proprietorship by default, since they did not bother to form any other business entity. **A sole proprietorship is THE ABSOLUTE WORST business entity!**

(a) It provides absolutely no legal protection— if

someone sues you and wins, they can take everything you have worked so hard for, including your house, cars & your baby's sippy cup!

(b) Any profit from a sole proprietorship is subject to an additional 15% self-employment tax that could be avoided simply by choosing a different entity. The TaxSavers were paying **UNNECESSARY TAXES!** Why would you pay tax that you don't have to pay? A supreme court justice (Judge Learned Hand) said "anyone may arrange his affairs so that his taxes shall be as low as possible; he is not bound to choose that pattern which best pays the treasury. There is not even a patriotic duty to increase one's taxes."

(c) In addition and most importantly, the tax form used for a sole proprietorship–schedule C–is **the most audited form at the IRS**. Just because you have a schedule C, the IRS is looking at your return a little closer. Believe me, you really don't want that! This reason alone should convince you to stop being a sole proprietor.

Mr. TaxSaver receives a 1099-Miscellaneous form from the main company every year for around $500,000. Zero taxes have been paid on this money and it is charged to Mr. TaxSaver's social security number.

My recommendation was to form two (2) corporations. The first one would be designated as an S-corporation for Mr. TaxSaver since he receives the 1099-M for $500,000. An S-corporation is not subjected to the additional 15% tax on profits (self employment tax) that a sole proprietorship pays. So right off the bat, we are saving 15% taxes on the business' annual profit!

I recommended a C corporation for Mrs. TaxSaver because she has long dreamed of owning her own catering service. Since the main business hosts several weekly meetings in the TaxSaver's home to recruit new business associates, it is the perfect opportunity for Mrs. TaxSaver to showcase her culinary skills by providing refreshments for the meetings. Mrs. TaxSaver hopes the meetings will be a source of catering leads. But in the meantime, the C-corporation serves a tri-fold purpose in tax planning: (a) by creating a deduction for the main company— payment for catering services rendered, (b) a vehicle through which she can hire their children and (c) an entity that can support a Medical Expense Reimbursement Plan. (Stay tuned...this will be explained later.)

2) **OFFICE SPACE:** The TaxSavers operate their business out of their home. I recommended they use their basement as office space. This would give them a hefty deduction for office space since they would depreciate 1/3 of their $700,000 home on their taxes every year. The corporation will pay the TaxSavers rent in the amount of $2500/mo, the going rate in their area for a space that size. This generates a deduction of $30,000 a year! (*Note:* The TaxSavers must claim this amount as rental income on their personal taxes,

but against it they will write off expenses for 1/3 of the house, including mortgage, utilities, property taxes, repairs, etc.)

3) **AUTOMOBILE**: Both Mr. & Mrs. TaxSaver do a great deal of driving. They set up and attend numerous meetings to recruit new members 4-7 evenings a week. They estimate driving at least 100 miles each day. My recommendation is to set up an accountable plan which serves a 2-fold purpose: It reimburses them for mileage at the current mileage rate—2010 rate is 50 cents per mile—which is TAX FREE money (meaning they don't have to report it on their taxes) and it gives the corporation a deduction of $18,250.

4) **PAY YOURSELF:** One of the biggest mistakes new business owners make is thinking they don't have to pay themselves a salary. They think it's ok to take money out of the business account to pay their personal expenses. They also think are avoiding the self employment tax. (This is the payroll tax you would have paid had received a W-2.) Well believe me, you aren't getting away with anything. The IRS has already decided what business owners who do what you do should make, and if you are audited, they will assess you that amount and charge you the payroll taxes, late fees, penalties and interest for not paying in a timely manner. Because of their specific duties in the business, I recommended Mr. TaxSaver take a salary of $85,000 and Mrs. TaxSaver take a salary of $55,000.

5) **PAY YOUR FAMILY:** The TaxSavers don't give their

kids allowance anymore, they pay salaries and write it off on their taxes! They have a son in college and a daughter in private school – who both help host the 3-5 business meetings held in their home each week. The kids prepare and serve food, run the projector, pass out product samples and clean up after the affair. I recommended a salary of $300/week for each of them – which is $15,600/year. The TaxSavers are happy to get a tax deduction of $31,200 for the money they were giving their kids anyway. (Tax court has upheld that children as young as age 7 can work! Just be sure to keep time sheets, record duties and I recommend signing an employment agreement as well.)

Another benefit is the college-age child now qualifies for financial aid as an independent student. The TaxSavers no longer claim him as a dependent on their taxes, he files his own tax return. When the TaxSavers were claiming him as a dependent, he did not receive any financial aid because the TaxSaver's income was so high. But as an independent student, he is now receiving financial aid benefits.

The daughter in private school uses her salary to pay her $1000/month tuition – while the remainder is split between a Roth IRA which will be used for college tuition, her savings account and her pocket for spending money.

The TaxSavers also have a 14-year-old who built and hosts their website. He also maintains their email marketing and customer retention programs. I recommended a salary of $400/week to be split between (a) his pocket—spending money (b) 529 education plan—college savings plan and (c) Roth IRA and (d) his savings account. Total deduction annual: $20,800 .

6) **MEDICAL EXPENSES:** Since the TaxSaver's income is so high, they have not been able to deduct medical expenses on their personal tax return. The rule is medical expenses must be more than 7.5% of their income. (If 7.5% of their income was $10,000 and they had $10,001 in medical expenses, they would get credit for $1.) So I recommended setting up a medical expense reimbursement plan (MERP) – which would allow them to write off all of their medical expenses, including health insurance premiums, prescriptions, co-pays, braces, exams, therapy, etc. Each time they have a medical expense, they simply submit their receipt to the company, which in turn reimburses the TaxSavers. Last year's medical expenses for the family of 6 was $12,529. This reimbursement is tax free money that they do not have to report on their tax return!

7) **Retirement Plan: My tax plann**ing service includes a visit with a Certified Financial Planner who assesses the family's financial goals and retirement needs, then structures a plan to meet those goals. The most favorable plan for the TaxSavers was a 401(K) plan which would allow each spouse to contribute $16,500 each year plus 25% of their income. Their retirement plan results in a deduction of $68,000.

8) **DayCare:** With one child in daycare, the TaxSavers

paid almost $7000 in child care fees last year and received absolutely no credit on their tax return. A Dependant Care Reimbursement Account allows them a maximum deduction of $5000 each year. The TaxSavers have the money deducted from their salary and every week after they pay daycare fees, submit the receipt and are reimbursed 100% on a tax-free basis from the money set aside in their account.

9) **Athletic Facility:** Since the TaxSavers have a pool, trampoline, a basketball/tennis court and exercise equipment on the business premises (at home), and all employees (the family) have access to it, they can write off the repair, maintenance and purchase of equipment as an athletic facility. Last years' expenses were $2,820.

10) **Equipment/furniture Leasing:** Mr.TaxSaver purchased all the equipment and furniture the business uses. The business can then rent the equipment and furniture on a monthly basis from Mr. TaxSaver. Based on local rental company rates, he is able to charge $1970 a month which results in a deduction of $23,640. He will need to claim this income on his personal tax return, but against it we will write off the depreciation, maintenance and repair of the equipment and furniture.

THE RESULTS:

a. Home Office..............................$30,000
b. Automobile $18,250
c. Salary for Owners $140,000
d. Salary for Children $52,000
e. Medical Expenses $12,529

f. Retirement Plan $68,000

g. Daycare $5,000

h. Athletic Facility $2,820

i. Equipment Leasing $23,640

Total : $352,239

TAXABLE INCOME IS REDUCED BY $352,239!

After deducting the normal business expenses the TaxSavers have reduced their taxable income to $0!

The TaxSavers now operate their business tax free!

It is very important to have all your i's dotted and your t's crossed when it comes to substantiating documentation for the Internal Revenue Service. All of your paperwork must conform to IRS guidelines, be accurate and in place, in order for you to claim the deductions. You must also adopt any of the measures you choose to use through a meeting of your Board of Directors.

It is vitally important to keep receipts, mileage logs, and actually write checks from the company to yourself to substantiate expenses and create a paper trail. The best strategy is to hire a professional bookkeeper/accountant that understands your tax planning strategy to keep your books and paperwork in order.

For questions about tax planning, please feel free to contact me at: larisa@abundantreturns.com.

ABOUT LARISA

I Paid More Taxes Than a Billionaire!!

I started Abundant Returns Tax Service back in 1991 after seeing on TV that Ross Perot, then presidential candidate and CEO of a multi-billion dollar corporation, **paid less than $2000 in personal income taxes!**

I just couldn't believe it because…

I made $35,000 that year and paid _More Than $4000_ in federal taxes alone!!!

I paid **more than double** the taxes a Billionaire paid!!!

I was flabbergasted to say the least.

"He's a billionaire," I kept saying to myself. "How is it legal for me to pay more taxes than a billionaire?"

I kept tossing it around in my head. I just couldn't believe it. I worried about how I was going to pay the rent. I struggled to buy a bus pass every week. I had to make "arrangements" every month to pay my utility bills. My grocery budget was $15/week and I was paying more income taxes than a billionaire?!!!

It made absolutely no sense to me. It still makes no sense to me…20 years later! (If I think about it long enough, I still get mad.)

This was an "a-ha" moment for me—a life lesson that shattered my very sheltered view of reality. I learned two very valuable lessons— life is not fair and rich people can avoid income taxes.

So I got busy.

I took several income tax preparation courses.

I read hundreds of books on taxes. I've prepared thousands of tax returns.

I worked for the IRS and a local tax office. I learned about taxes and how to use the tax law to my advantage. I learned how to live "tax free" like billionaires do.

Now I'm ready to share that knowledge with you so you can "Keep More Money In Your Pocket" too. In my ebook, "Pay Yourself Instead of Uncle Sam", I explore many tax strategies that will help you reduce your taxes as low as possible. You can find it at http://small-business-tax-info.com.

For special offers to readers of this book and to join my mailing list, go to: http://small-business-tax-info.com/breakingthecode. You can contact me at: larisa@abundantreturns.com or feel free to give me a call at: (770) 451-6330.

CHAPTER 7

BREAKING THE TAX CODE

– EAT, DRINK, BE MERRY
– AND DOCUMENT, DOCUMENT, DOCUMENT

BY GARY D. HELDT, JR., CPA

"You must pay taxes. But there's no law that says you gotta leave a tip."
~ Morgan Stanley advertisement

I f you own your own business, you understand that there are times where it's absolutely essential to wine and dine clients – and even entertain your own employees with a summer picnic or holiday party.

Believe it or not, the IRS understands that too. They know

that sometimes, a critical part of doing business is *not* to do business – and to instead entertain important customers by taking them to a basketball game or some other event.

Unfortunately, there's something else the IRS knows – and that's the fact that the Meals and Entertainment business deduction is one of the most widely abused deductions on tax returns.

That's why the Meals and Entertainment deduction has some of the most stringent rules and regulations regarding what's allowable and what's not. And also why you're only allowed to deduct 50% of them in most cases.

Yes, I said "most." Many taxpayers are unaware that there are certain instances where you can actually write off the entire cost of a meal or party provided to employees or clients.

When you plan accordingly and set up your events, entertainment and meals to be as IRS-friendly as possible, you can save a lot on your taxes – *and* have a good time. In this chapter, we're going to talk about how to maximize your Meal and Entertainment deductions and also about how to make sure your M&E deductions are as "audit-proof" as possible.

AN M&E CASE STUDY

When you *don't* make the effort to protect your M&E deductions from an audit, you could be in for a lot of grief – and possibly a lot of extra taxes.

I can illustrate just that scenario by relating the story of a client who was referred to me for help. He was a real estate broker who was in the midst of a large-scale audit. The IRS auditor was very severe – and was threatening to disallow ALL of his M&E deductions, which were very large. If that happened, my new client was going to owe the IRS an extra $30,000 – not a happy prospect.

The big problem the real estate broker had was the lack of proper documentation. While he had receipts from most of his M&E expenses and was able to get the ones he was missing from credit card statements, he did not keep track of the business purpose of the expenses, where they occurred or the names of the clients he was entertaining.

The IRS requires that this basic information ("who, where and why") be kept either in a log or written on the back of the receipts in question. They also require it be recorded in a timely manner – if you can't do it within 24 hours of the M&E expense, then it at least has to be recorded in a weekly log.

That meant, technically, my new client couldn't regroup and simply try to supply that information from memory.

Fortunately, what he *did* have was an appointment book, with the "who," "where" and sometimes even the "why" already written down for most of the M&E expenses. And these appointments were obviously recorded close to the actual events in question, so they passed the "timely manner" test.

We used the appointment book and all the receipts to then put together an "entertainment book" for the auditor, with complete documentation of all the deductions that the broker listed on his tax return.

But the auditor, who was a little green, still fought us on many issues.

For example, because the broker represented many properties, he would invite other real estate agents over to his house and present a slide show of the properties to them. By doing this at home, rather than holding individual open houses at the actual properties, he saved a lot of time and money. Naturally, he would serve the agents some food and drink at the slide show at his home.

The auditor felt like he was trying to get away with charging off parties at his house that weren't business-related. Fortunately, the broker had the slide shows in question, photos of the agents at the slide shows, the guest lists for these events and the receipts for the food and beverage. The auditor had to allow the deduction, as we simply had too much proof that it was business-oriented.

The broker also held a large holiday party at his home, where he invited everyone that had bought a home from him or had referred new clients during the past year. Again, the auditor thought it was a personal party that the IRS didn't really have to cover. Again, the broker had substantial evidence that it was all about business, including a copy of the actual invitation that was sent to clients which specifically indicated it was a business gathering. The auditor ended up allowing that deduction as well.

Finally, the broker had also deducted expenses for playing golf with clients as well as taking them to football games –

he had season tickets for one team. The auditor also tried to say they weren't relevant to his business. However, the IRS guidelines specifically state that you are allowed to entertain a client in this manner as long as you discuss business before the entertainment takes place. In all cases, the broker entertained these clients after business meetings – he had all the meetings documented in his appointment book – so the deductions were allowed.

Well, *almost* all of them. The broker wanted to deduct the entire cost of the season football tickets. The auditor ruled (and rightly so) that the broker had to break down the cost of the tickets per individual game – and could only write off the games he used to entertain business clients.

The end result of all this work? My client the real estate broker now only owed the IRS $5000 after the audit, instead of $30,000 – which he could live with.

HELPING BUSINESSES FIND THEIR TAX ADVANTAGE

You can see from the above story just how important it is to have the right person behind you when you face a situation with the IRS.

Although we provide a wide range of financial, accounting and tax services to our clients, nothing pleases me more than personally helping a client like that real estate broker, and providing the best service possible at the fairest possible price. It's why I became an accountant in the first place.

My mom was a single parent and schoolteacher who raised me and my two sisters on her own. When I was in high school, she was finally able to buy a house. Because of this new and potentially complex financial situation, she thought it best to have her taxes done by a professional for that first year of home ownership, instead of doing the return on her own as she had in previous years.

When I found out the accountant she hired had charged her $350 (and this was a few years ago, remember) for what was still a relatively simple tax return, I was outraged and was sure she had been taken advantage of. And I decided then and there to go to school, learn accounting and not take advantage of people who hired me.

The next day, I signed up for bookkeeping class. I got a lot of looks, being 6'3" and a football player – not the usual candidate for accounting. But it was amazing – I took to it like a duck to water. It was almost second nature to me.

After my education, I worked for both for-profit companies and nonprofits, learning the ropes. My goal was to gain a wide range of experience so I could work with all kinds of businesses when I went on my own.

That happened in 1999, when I bought an existing accounting practice. We started with 140 personal tax clients and 75 business clients. Since then, we've built those numbers up to about 775 personal and 200 business clients. And we did it all through word-of-mouth. Up until last year, we did no advertising or marketing of any kind.

One of the secrets of our success is that we have a very

strong, secure website that our clients can access 24/7. They can upload their documents through a secure portal, or download information and work we've completed for them as well. This allows us to work with clients all over the country and even all over the world. We have many clients in the military – some even sending us their tax information from a submarine somewhere in the Pacific.

We also work hard at maintaining a close relationship with our clients. In addition to checking in with them regularly, we also put out a monthly newsletter, that features a column written by my son, Tyler. Actually, since *"Tyler's Corner"* began when he was a newborn, he doesn't *really* write it...but some of our clients have threatened to fire us if we ever stop printing it! I don't think they'd really leave us, but you never know...

Finally, we think it's important to give back to the community. We formed a business referral group in our area – where trusted firms can recommend each other when clients need a different product or service to what our individual companies offer. We also founded a nonprofit charity called *"For the Kids."* For the past 11 years, *For the Kids* has organized a charity golf tournament where we raise money for a seriously ill child. In 2010, we were fortunate enough to be able to donate over $21,000 to a local family in need of the money for medical bills.

I believe there is a certain level of service you should be able to expect from anyone that you hire to do your tax planning – and I make sure to provide that same level to my clients. Here are three things to look for:

- **The top person at the firm should be available to you.**

  I make myself available to any of our clients if they really need to talk to me; I don't hide in my office. I believe in service to the point where we *underpromise* and *overdeliver*. That's how I would've liked my mom to be treated.

- **Your accountant should contact you for regular updates.**

  We try to connect with all our clients on a monthly basis so we know what's going on with their finances and how they might want to handle things for their next tax return.

- **Your accountant should be helping you plan in advance for the next tax year.**

  If you plan now, you can often plot out significant tax advantages by how you approach your finances. If you wait until it's April 15th, you're generally stuck with what you've done and there's not as much you can do to lower your taxes.

M&E TAX TIPS

The kind of planning I just spoke about really can help you save when it comes to Meals & Entertainment deductions. I'd like to close out this chapter with a few more tax tips on this deduction that you may not be aware of:

- If you give someone tickets to an event, it's better to take that as an entertainment deduction rather than a business gift deduction. That's because you can only write off $25 for any business gift, no matter what the actual cost.

- You *can* deduct the cost of entertaining your spouse and children in certain instances. The general rule of thumb is, if the client or business associate you're entertaining has their spouse and kids with them, it's reasonable for you to bring yours.

- You can deduct the cost of providing lunches for your staff – depending again on certain criteria. The tax code says if your employees have 45 minutes or less for their lunch break and there aren't enough eating establishments in the immediate area, this is allowable. But you must supply lunches for at least over half of the staff.

When you do supply meals to employees under the above conditions, you can deduct 100% of the cost, instead of just 50%. Here are a few more instances where that's the case:

TICKETS TO A CHARITABLE SPORTS EVENT

Remember that charity golf tournament that our nonprofit company holds every year earlier? Well, if you brought a client to it, the cost of the tickets would be 100% deductible.

FOOD AT THE OFFICE

The IRS allows employers to deduct 100% of the expense of stocking the office kitchen for employees. Coffee, soft drinks, and other snacks and beverages bought to be consumed on the business premises all qualify.

EMPLOYEE PARTIES

Whether it's a holiday party, a summer office barbeque or a company awards banquet, it's 100% deductible – as are all recreational, social and/or entertainment gatherings that are primarily for the benefit of *all* employees – *not* just the executive suite!

MEALS FOR THE PUBLIC

Maybe, to promote your new Jiffy Lube, you decide to give away free hot dogs on a Saturday afternoon. Those dogs (and all the trimmings) are 100% deductible – as is any food you give away to whoever shows up. The trick here is that they are actually considered *advertising* expenses.

FOOD AND BEVERAGE FOR A SALES SEMINAR

If you hold a sales seminar, and you have snacks and drinks for the attendees, the cost again is 100% deductible. That's because they come under the cost of the actual seminar and are *not* considered part of the Meals & Entertainment deduction.

CONCLUSION – DOCUMENTATION & PLANNING

Remember always to document the "who, what and where" of M&E expenses. You also don't need to hold on to receipts for less than $75, but you should note the expense in a log, along with the necessary business substantiation.

Lastly, always keep up to date with the latest IRS regulations. Changes to the tax code are made frequently by Congress, so consult with your tax professional or accountant – so you can do your tax planning with the correct information.

When you adhere to the IRS regulations and do the necessary documentation, you can enjoy a big Meals & Entertainment deduction without having to sweat the threat of an audit. After all, Meals & Entertainment should be the fun part of running a business – so enjoy yourself and enjoy saving on your tax bill!

ABOUT GARY

Gary D. Heldt, Jr., is a Certified Public Accountant. Gary owns and operates **Small Business Advisors**, in Gambrills, Maryland. Small Business Advisors serves a client base from the Baltimore, MD, Washington, DC and Northern Virginia vicinity, and holds the title of Premier Tax Coach in Anne Arundel County, Maryland.

Gary acquired Small Business Advisors in 1999. Prior to that, however, and subsequent to his graduation from Shepherd College, and with an Accounting education under his belt, Gary's focus was to gain a wide range of experience with his Accounting knowledge, working in both the for-profit and non-profit industries. This foundation within these industries, combined with the desire to provide the best service possible at the fairest possible price, led Gary to open his own business doing just that in 1999.

Since 1999, Gary has grown Small Business Advisors by five times its acquired size, and maintained a retention rate of 94% while doing so. A majority of this growth was through word-of-mouth. Up until last year, there was no advertising or marketing of any kind. Maintaining a close relationship with clients, including checking in with them regularly, resulted in this successful growth.

Gary's clients rely upon his competent and experienced advice. Gary's clients receive total financial services, whether they are individuals, large or small businesses, or other types of businesses and agencies. Gary is dedicated to the three underlying principles of professionalism, responsiveness and quality. Gary's reputation for providing quality service reflects the high standards he demands of himself. His high standards, responsive service and specialized staff, spell the difference between Small Business Advisors and "the rest".

Gary also believes that it is important to give back to the community. He helped form a business referral group where trusted firms recommend each other when their own clients need a different product or service that they themselves cannot provide. Gary and Small Business Advisors also helped found a non-profit charity called "For The Kids", and for the past 11 years, this charity has organized a charity golf tourna-ment where funds are raised for seriously ill children. In 2010 alone, the charity was fortunate enough to be able to donate over $21,000 to a local family in need of money for medical bills.

Gary Heldt, Jr., CPA and Small Business Advisors are more than "just Accountants".

CHAPTER 8

TAX SHELTERS

BY JAMES (JIM) HENDERSON, CPA

Webster defines a Tax Shelter as "a strategy, invest-ment or tax code provision that reduces tax liabil-ity." Tax shelter investments were extremely popular when the maximum federal tax rate was 70% and above. Wealthy individuals were looking for ways to dramatically reduce their tax burden. Currently, the maximum federal rate stands at about half of the 70% figure. Combine this with the passage of the 1986 Tax Reform Act which dramatically limited tax losses from passive activities, and the tax shelter went the way of the Dodo Bird and the Sony Walkman.

There still exists, however, strategies and tax code provi-sions which can save any taxpayer significant tax dollars. These Tax Shelters are not just available for the wealthy, as almost anyone with a little proper advanced planning can avail themselves of their benefits.

I have been asked, "How can I save $100,000 in taxes?" Now it's pretty rare where one can save that amount in one transaction. However, much like the answer to the question "How do you eat an elephant?" ...the response "One bite at a time!" applies. Given the multitude of Tax Shelters available and being utilized over one's lifetime, tax savings of $100,000 and even more can easily be attained.

PEOPLE DON'T PLAN FOR FAILURE, THEY JUST FAIL TO PLAN!

One would think the logical next step would be to start researching all Tax Shelters. That would be like checking out all the homes available for sale around the world when you know you want a three-bedroom, two-bathroom condominium in Boston served by public transportation in the $400,000 range. The real first step to finding what Tax Shelters would be best for you is to know your Financial Plan.

What is your Financial Plan? In its most basic terms, it is the profile of where you are at versus where you want to be. It consists of both your cash inflows and outflows, as well as what you own and what you owe. Therefore, in order to get from your present profile point to a future profile point, you need a Financial Plan that is specifically tailored to your circumstances.

The first step to determine your current profile would be to gather your financial records, such as check registers, bank statements, brokerage statements, retirement accounts, property listings, insurance policies, credit card records, mortgage and other loan statements, etc. From these you can clearly determine where your inflows come from and where the outflows go. You can get a snapshot of what you own vs. what you owe. Hopefully you own more than you owe.

With this information, you can project where you want to be at some future point, then implement plans of action to get there. Examples would be: Pay off mortgage in 15 years, … have $500k in retirement by age 65, …buy a vacation home by age 45, … save $125k for college for each child.

THE TAX MAN COMETH...

Financial Plans involve financial transactions, and it is a fact of life that in almost every financial transaction, taxes rear their ugly head. In fact, taxes can amount to 50% or more of a transaction's cost. If you reduce or eliminate the taxes, you keep more money in your pocket. Therefore, for each of your financial transactions, you have to identify the Tax Shelter (i.e., the strategy or tax code) which will save you tax dollars.

Now, how do you determine what you will save? You must know your marginal tax bracket. First, your marginal bracket is not the same as your average tax rate. Indeed, someone's average federal and state income tax rate could be 18% of total income, but their marginal rate is always higher, say 33%. Your marginal tax rate is how much your taxes will change for every marginal increase or decrease in income. So, even if you have an average tax rate of 18%, but a marginal rate of 33%, you know that an additional $3,000 of interest income will not cost you $540 in taxes, but close to $1,000.

Secondly, your marginal tax rate is not always just comprised of your federal and state income taxes. Other taxes could come into play. These include, among others, Social Security and Medicare taxes on wages (7.65% up to certain limits), self-employment taxes on unincorporated business earned income (15.3%) up to certain limits, penalties on premature retirement plan distributions (10% or more, depending on plan type), the Alternative Minimum Tax, and lower taxes on long-term capital gains and qualified dividends (currently maxed at 15%).

Thirdly, your marginal tax rate is always subject to change, depending on the year, the tax laws currently in effect, and your income level and type.

Lastly, you should look at the marginal tax rate not only for yourself, but for all members of your immediate family. A child's marginal tax rate, even after factoring in the provisions of the Kiddie Tax, can be much lower than that of a parent. Thus, shifting income to a child could save significant taxes for the family unit.

To keep it simple, we'll just deal with the following marginal tax rate assumptions:

	Combined (Rounded)
Federal income tax 28% and State income tax 5%	33%
Social Security/Medicare 7.65%	40%
Self-Employment 15.3%	48%

Since most taxpayers can count earned wages as a major inflow, let's look at Tax Shelters that may be available to them.

RETIRE IN STYLE

A large number of employers offer retirement plans, some even with company-match provisions. If your employer does not offer one, you can open up an IRA (Individual Retirement Account) on your own. As part of your Financial Plan, you want to retire some day and have enough money to live on, so a retirement account would fit the bill.

Let's say you want to save $100/week towards retirement. Doing this on your own, you would have to earn about $150/week to net $100/week after taxes assuming a 33% marginal tax rate. To add insult to injury, you would be taxed on the annual earnings on the investment account. Not a very good deal.

On the other hand, let's say your employer has a 401(k) retirement plan with an annual match of up to $1,000. If you placed $150/week into the plan, your net paycheck would remain the same as outlined above as if you would have saved $100/week after taxes. However, at the end of the year, you would have $8,800 in your 401(k) plan (52 x $150 + $1,000) vs. $5,200 in the investment account ($52 x $100), a $3,600 or over 67% increased annual savings benefit.

Contributions and earnings thereon within the retirement plan will grow tax-deferred until withdrawn. The normal assumption is that you will have a lower marginal tax rate when retired than during your working years. If you feel that your marginal tax rate may be the same or even higher when you are retired, then you may want to consider a Roth IRA. While you get no current deduction, contributions and earnings thereon will be tax-free if withdrawn during retirement.

The main reasons I like employer-sponsored plans are:

1. Funding is done at the payroll source, so funds are never available to you. I've always found that an individual's spending expands or contracts depending on the funds available. Therefore, the best laid plans of saving on your own can and usually do go awry.
2. You retain control of all your funds, rather than having a portion gone to the government via taxes.
3. With control come options. While funds should be used for retirement, in emergency or financial crisis situations, the funds are available through loan or withdrawal. While taxes and penalties could ensue, better to have the fund availability option than nothing at all.

LOAD UP AT THE CAFETERIA

Another Tax Shelter benefit for wage-earners would be employer-sponsored cafeteria plans. Under such pans, employees can select from a smorgasbord of benefits, most on a pre-tax basis. Choices would include health and dental insurance, medical and dependent care assistance plans (DCAP).

There is a lot of misinformation out there about these plans, so much so that people are not participating when they really should. I've heard things like "I can deduct medical anyway, why do I need to join the plan?" or "I can get the child care credit, so why do I need the DCAP?" or "my wife's hairdresser said it was a bad idea."

While there may be a small portion of truth in the above (except for the hairdresser's opinion), the full truth is that you will usually save much more in taxes by participating than not. Take medical expenses for example. While it is true that medical costs are indeed deductible, they are only allowable as itemized deductions and only if all medical costs presently exceed 7.5% of adjusted gross income which, in my experience, is very rare.

So, if you participated and had $5,000 in health insurance and out-of-pocket medical, you would save 40% (federal, state, Social Security and Medicare) in taxes, or $2,000. In the vast majority of cases, little or no tax savings would result if you tried to deduct medical as an itemized deduction.

By contributing $5,000 to a DCAP to be used towards Junior's pre-school tuition to allow you and your spouse to work would save the family unit the same 40% in taxes or $2,000. Claiming the child care credit for one child on your tax return usually results in only a $600 tax savings, or $1,400 less.

USING YOUR SHELTER AS A TAX SHELTER

The number one tax shelter for most taxpayers results from

home ownership. The federal tax code and some states will allow deductions for home mortgage interest and real estate taxes. Absent these deductions, taxpayers who rent their homes normally take the standard deduction in computing their taxes.

Taxpayers are allowed to take the higher of the standard deduction or their itemized deductions. Itemized deductions include: Medical, Taxes, Interest, Contributions, Casualty & Theft Losses, Job Related Costs and Miscellaneous. For further details as to what are included as itemized deductions, please refer to the IRS web site at www.irs.gov

This site contains a wealth of information for this and other tax inquiries you may have.

To demonstrate the tax savings a single or married taxpayer could attain through home ownership is outlined below based on the following assumptions (obviously results will vary, based on your particular circumstances and tax year):

Single individual, earning $55,000, buying a condominium for $150,000 and financing $120,000.

Married individuals, combined earnings of $100,000, buying a home for $275,000 and financing $220,000.

	Single	Married
Mortgage interest	$6,600	$12,050
Real Estate taxes	2,700	4,300
State income tax	2,500	4,500
Contributions and other	1,200	2,100
Total itemized	13,000	22,950
Standard deduction	5,800	9,750
Excess deductions	7,200	13,200
Marginal Tax Rate Bracket	33%	33%
Tax Savings Per Year	2,400	4,400
Tax Savings Per Month	$200	$367

Not only do you get tax benefits while owning a home, but a husband and wife can get up to a $500k gain exclusion when they sell their home in the future. This gain exclusion provision could save you about $100k in taxes!

HOME IS WHERE THE OFFICE IS

If you are required to maintain a home office as a condition of employment, or you are self-employed and work out of your home as your principle place of business, you may be allowed a home office deduction. You may think that it may not make much of a difference as the major home deductions of mortgage interest and real estate taxes are already allowed as itemized deductions. While this is true, all the other home ownership costs (including repairs, maintenance, insurance, utilities, depreciation, condo fees, etc.) would now move into the deduction calculation column. Additionally, the portion of your mortgage interest and real estate taxes related to the home office could save you an additional 15.3% in taxes if you are self-employed.

Let's say that you have a qualifying home office and $10,000 of previously non-deductible home ownership costs. If you use 15% of your home for business, then roughly $1,500 of additional deductions would be allowed on your return. This could save you roughly $500 as an employee, or roughly $720 as a self-employed individual.

IT'S A FAMILY AFFAIR

It has been shown that raising a child to age 18 could cost upwards of $250k, and paying for four years of college could set you back another $250k. So, for the potential $500k investment, you should be able to get some tax benefits in return. The tax code is friendly where dependent children are involved. The myriad of benefits include dependency deduction, child tax credit, child care credit, adoption credit, education tax credits and deductions, college 529 savings plans, earned income credit, etc. While these may seem like a lot, and I am not minimizing their benefits, the simple fact is that you will not come anywhere close to recouping your $500k.

An often overlooked planning tool is utilizing dependents lower tax brackets. This works with earned income (i.e., wages), but does not fully work for unearned income because of the applicability of the Kiddie Tax for dependent children. Still, under present law, the first $950 of unearned income could be tax free, and the next $950 could then be taxed at the dependent's lower tax rate.

Therefore, a gifting program to move assets to the next generation could save the family some significant tax dollars. However, this strategy could backfire if you think you will be eligible for college financial aid. Assets in a child's name are assessed at a higher percentage in the financial aid formula than assets in a parent's name. This generally would reduce your aid eligibility.

PRACTICE NEPOTISM

If you have your own small closely-held business, like I do, then you almost always have your children help out with various business tasks. Whether it's stamping and sealing envelopes and cleaning the office at a young age, to doing more complex tasks as they mature, children can be a valuable asset to any thriving business. Some of you may now be saying "and the best part, ...they are free!" I want you to rethink that because you may be giving away tax dollars needlessly.

Let's say you are self-employed. You have 2 children and set aside $50 a week for each of them for allowance, spending money or savings. In order to have, after taxes, $100 available weekly, or $5,200 per year, you would have to earn $10,000 per year. Indeed you would lose $4,800 to taxes at a 48% rate (Federal, State and Self-Employment).

Instead, what if you put each of your children on the payroll for $5,000 each per year? These wages would reduce your annual taxable income by $10,000, thus saving you the aforementioned $4,800 in taxes. Now you may be saying, "what about payroll taxes the business would have to pay on the wages, and the income taxes your children would have to pay on their earnings?"

If your children are less than 18 years old and work for their parents in an unincorporated business, then they are not subject to social security and medicare taxes, for either the employee or employer portions. Additionally they are not subject to federal unemployment and most state unemployment and other assessments.

Well what about income taxes for the children? As their wages are earned income and not subject to the Kiddie Tax, they can each utilize their standard deduction, currently $5,800, to reduce taxable income to zero. So as long as their total income is less than the standard deduction, they pay no federal income tax, and in most cases, would not be subject to state income tax.

ROTH IRA vs. COLLEGE 529 SAVINGS PLANS

Some may think that it would be best to take some or all of the money earned by the children in the above example and place it in a College 529 Savings Plan. While I truly like these plans, they may not be the best investment in this particular circumstance, and could actually cause some unintended negative consequences. A better choice could be a Roth IRA in the child's name. Here's why.

529 Plans are similar to Roths in that they both offer tax

deferred growth and tax free treatment if funds are used for their stated purposes. So if you use the 529 plan funds for qualified education expenses, the earnings are tax free. Roth distributions in retirement are likewise tax free.

What if 529 funds are not used for their stated purpose? Let's say Junior gets a full scholarship, or Junior is not the college type and starts his own business after high school, or Junior works, stays home and takes night classes at the inexpensive community college? If the 529 funds are taken out for non-educational purposes, then not only would the account earnings be taxable, but also would be subject to a 10% penalty tax. Not a good result.

Also, if you qualify for financial aid, savings in 529 plans actually count against you and reduce your financial aid award. Additionally, any funds from a 529 plan used for educational costs render those same costs ineligible for any education credit or deduction tax benefit.

Instead, let's say that you put up to $5,000 (the Roth annual limit) into each child's Roth account. Later, the account principle can be withdrawn for college costs without any tax consequence. If the earnings are then withdrawn for college, they will be taxed, however they will not be subject to the 10% Roth penalty tax on early distributions as paying for college costs is one of the penalty exceptions.

As retirement funds are usually not an assessable asset for financial aid purposes, funding a Roth IRA should not hurt you from a financial aid standpoint. Using Roth funds should not affect your eligibility for any education credit or deduction tax benefit.

Lastly, if the Roth funds are not needed for college, then they can be retained and used for other purposes, such as buying a home, later higher education costs, retirement, etc., with little or no tax or penalty cost if proper planning is employed. Principal withdrawals will generally always be tax-free.

GIMME SHELTER!

So in conclusion, if you have a Financial Plan and truly understand the tax implications of each financial transaction that are part of your plan, then you will go a long way to minimizing the potentially largest financial transaction cost, namely taxes. Every tax dollar saved stays in your pocket to be used as you desire. *Remember, tax evasion is a crime, tax avoidance is just plain smart.*

The tax strategies above are presented to demonstrate the potential savings which can be attained. As everyone's circumstance is different, I would strongly recommend that you consult a qualified professional who can help you with your plan. Trying to do it on your own would be just plain dumb, and the consequences dire.

ABOUT JIM

"More than a Bean Counter"

Most CPAs and other tax advisors operate in the after-the-fact world. Much like a score keeper in a baseball game, they can tell you what has happened, but have almost no input on making something happen.

Today more than ever individuals and small business owners need a true "Tax Bench Coach" to provide proper pro-active planning services. When one considers that taxes can claim up to 50% of any planned financial transaction, operating without knowing the tax ramifications, or without a viable tax minimization strategy, is just plain stupid.

James (Jim) Henderson, CPA is a graduate of the prestigious Boston Latin School, attended the University of Notre Dame, and graduated with high distinction from Babson College. He is a licensed CPA, Real Estate Broker and Notary Public. He has attended and presented numerous seminars on tax planning, real estate and home ownership, college planning, retirement planning, QuickBooks and other topics of interest to his clients and associates.

Jim, officially known as James A. Henderson, CPA, is the founder of Henderson, Grealis & Associates, PC CPA (aka *TaxSense*) with four offices in the Boston area. In addition to pro-active tax planning services, the firm, as Certified QuickBooks Pro Advisors, assists clients in making sense out of their numbers. "Information is power. Without *20/20* current and accurate financial statements, one cannot see where they've been, never mind see where they are going. As a result, proper tax planning becomes virtually impossible".

To learn more about Jim, please visit: TaxSense.com or contact him at (888) TAX-SENSE.

CHAPTER 9

THE TAX SAVVY DIVORCE

BY GARY D. KANE, CPA, MSA

You and your spouse have decided that you no longer want to be married to each other. What are the things that you are concerned about?   ...division of assets, child custody issues, alimony or maybe how you can prevent your spouse from getting an even piece of the marital pie. If you're like most people, income taxes are one of the last things that you consider if you consider them at all. Journalist and author, Nora Ephron once quipped, "Marriage is temporary but divorce is forever." The tax mistakes you make today will follow you for years to come. There are tax traps for the unwary and opportunities for the informed. The following are the six tax-savvy items to remember if you join the 50% of Americans who end up in family court.

1. ALIMONY IS DEDUCTIBLE AS LONG AS IT'S ALIMONY

The golden rule of divorce is that the spouse with 'the greatest amount of gold' gets to pay alimony. The computation of the amount and term of the alimony varies by state, but the tax rule is always the same: alimony is deductible by the payor and is includible in the income of the recipient. The definition of alimony is relatively straightforward: a cash payment paid pursuant to a decree of divorce or separate maintenance that will terminate on the death of the payee. The decree cannot state that the payment is not alimony and the parties cannot live together. As simple as the requirements are, it is not uncommon to find marital litigants and their representatives agreeing to terms that result in the law of unintended consequences. The common errors are:

  a. The payment doesn't terminate on death. Bad drafting by the lawyer that doesn't specifically state that the payments end on the death of the payee will result in the disallowance of the deduction. More often, the payee wants to make sure that, in the event of his or her death, the kids get the balance of the alimony award and will require that payments continue after the death of the payee with negative consequences to the payor. Since payments do not have to be made to the former spouse, payments on his or her behalf can be surprise alimony. For example, it is common for the court to order the husband to pay the former wife's mortgage payments. If the decree doesn't specifically exclude the payment from the computation of alimony, it is deductible by the former husband and income to the former wife.

b. Child support is not alimony and is not deductible. Payments disguised as alimony but are actually child support will, in almost all cases, fail the alimony test and not be deductible. If your goal is a tax deduction for the alimony, do not have the payment reduced based on a contingency related to the children such as their reaching the age of majority, finishing school, etc.

c. Unallocated support is generally alimony. Brad and Angie are getting divorced. The judge has ordered that Brad pay Angie $10,000 per month in temporary support, but Angie's lawyer doesn't request that the payment be allocated between deductible alimony and non-deductible child support. The result is that Brad gets a big deduction and Angie gets a new lawyer.

d. Don't forget alimony recapture. There is a provision in the code that eliminates the benefit of "front-loading" alimony, the purpose of which is to prevent the recasting of a property settlement as alimony. Formulas exist in the code to determine whether a greater portion of the alimony has been in the first three years after the divorce. If you fail the recapture test, the payor will be required to pay tax on the excess in the third year after the marriage. Likewise, the payee will get an offsetting deduction. For example, at the completion of the divorce, Brad pays Angie $150,000 and he decides to take an income tax deduction for the entire amount because his lawyer told him he could. His lawyer forgot to tell him that a little surprise awaited him when he filed his return three years later and had to pay it all back, and, if the tax rates go up in the interim, Brad is going to be really surprised.

2. LET YOUR 'EX' PAY THE TAX ON THE 401(K)

Distributions from a retirement account such as a 401(k) or an IRA are subject to tax and can be subject to a 10% penalty for early withdrawal. There are provisions in the Code that will allow the division of a retirement account in a divorce tax-free to the owner. A Qualified Domestic Relations Order or QDRO is an order by the court to pay a portion of the retirement account into the account of the former spouse or a dependent of the former spouse. If the rules are followed, the recipient will pay the tax on the distribution when it is paid. There is one other significant benefit to the use of a QDRO: a distribution to a former spouse or dependent, referred to as an alternate payee, will avoid the 10% penalty for early withdrawal of the funds from the account. So, for example, cash can be distributed to the alternate payee who may be in a lower tax bracket than the account owner. The net result is that a greater portion of the cash is available since the income tax paid is less and the 10% penalty is completely avoided. Even though the insertion of a QDRO is simple, the case law is replete with stories of people who liquidate their retirement accounts rather than ask their attorney to draft a QDRO. Not all lawyers are capable of drafting QDRO's but there are independent companies who prepare them.

3. YOU PAY FOR THEM, YOU DEDUCT THEM

The Internal Revenue Code provides for a deduction for each qualifying child. The Code also provides that in the case of divorced parents, the custodial parent gets the dependency exemption. The parent that has the child the greater portion of the year is considered to be the custodial parent. The IRS allows the custodial parent to release the claim to the exemption – by providing the non-custodial parent form 8332 or on a form that conforms to the designated IRS form. Nothing will substitute for the form 8332 or for a conforming agreement – not state law, not an order by the court and not even the faithful and timely payment of child support. The simple solution to this problem is to have the agreement affirmatively state that the non-custodial parent is entitled to the exemption for the children in language that conforms to the statute. The statement must, among other things, be signed by the custodial parent, specify the year or years for which the release is effective, state that the custodial parent will not claim the children and will not be conditioned on the payment of support or any other contingency. It must also provide for the name of the child, the year or years for which the claim is released, the name and social security number of the parents and it must be signed. Former spouses are generally more likely to sign an agreement at the completion of the divorce when there is a judge ordering them to sign. Once the ink is dry on the marital settlement agreement, the cost of obtaining a signature goes up dramatically. Thus, the best solution is to require the signature on the form when the final agreement is signed.

4. TAX ARBITRAGE

Arbitrage is the practice of taking advantage of a price difference between two or more markets in order to capitalize on the imbalance between the prices. The income tax rates are structured progressively, that is, as a taxpayer's income increases, he moves into higher tax brackets. So, for example, your first dollar of taxable income is taxed at 10% whereas the last dollar of taxable income might be taxed at a rate as high as 35%. For divorcing parties, the goal is to use the difference in the marginal rates to help pave the way for a settlement that is mutually beneficial. Alimony is usually paid by the spouse with the greater income. An experienced divorce lawyer or an accountant can compute the tax savings that can be used to help both parties meet their needs. The equitable distribution of the family's assets in a divorce can also be accomplished using the imbalance in the tax rates. The tax code provides that for purposes of determining gain or loss, the recipient of an asset received in a divorce settlement will have the same cost basis as the transferor. For purposes of the marital settlement, the current value is used to determine an equitable settlement. So high value, low cost assets can be given to the spouse with the smaller income and vice versa for the spouse with the greater income. For example, Brad gives Angie the $50,000 IRA which for income tax purposes is considered to have a zero cost basis. If Brad is in the 35% bracket and Angie is in the 15% bracket, the tax savings is $10,000 (35% minus 15% times $50,000) which is not a bad day at the track.

5.   DON'T TRUST THE JERK YOU JUST GOT RID OF

The story that most divorce lawyers hear on a regular basis from their clients is that their spouse is a thieving jerk (the TJ) who has been under-reporting his or her income for years. Then, after every issue in the divorce is settled, the TJ wants his or her 'ex' to sign a joint income tax return. The TJ even offers to sign an agreement holding the 'ex' harmless for any additional taxes that might be owed for any open year. If you file a joint income tax return with your spouse, you are jointly and severally liable for any taxes that are owed. But what happens if the former spouse has been a tax scofflaw who has grossly underreported his earnings or negligently failed to pay his tax obligation? The answer is that the IRS will attempt to collect the amount owed and will grab the money from you. So what should you do if you are faced with divorcing a thieving jerk? The obvious answer is to not file a joint return. The IRS is not bound by a *hold harmless* clause in a marital settlement agreement so your only option is to sue in family court to get your money back. Good luck with that strategy. DO NOT FILE A JOINT RETURN. The Jerk may have forged your name to a return which could be considered a validly filed joint return unless you immediately file a separate return and advise the IRS that your signature was forged. The final alternative is to seek *innocent spouse relief*. The Internal Revenue Code allows for you to divide your tax liability if you did not know and had no reason to know that the taxes were understated and it would be unfair to hold you responsible for the underpayment. In order to be granted *innocent spouse relief*, you have to file form 8857 with the IRS. Innocent spouse relief requires you to prove your case, and should only be used in cases where you violated the general rule.

Half of all marriages in the United States end up in divorce court and probably the majority of those are relatively straightforward. If you have substantial assets such as real estate or securities, an interest in a business or retirement plan or if your income is substantial enough to result in alimony, you should at a minimum seek out the advice of not only a seasoned divorce attorney, but also a CPA with experience in family law matters. Divorcing couples are dealing with emotional issues and cooler heads need to be involved. Remember the words of Nora Ephron and don't make a mistake that will haunt you forever.

ABOUT GARY

Gary D. Kane, CPA, MSA received his BSBA with honors with a major in accounting from the University of Florida and has a Master of Science in Accountancy from the University of Central Florida. He has over thirty-five years of public accounting experience – consisting of four years with the international accounting firm of Alexander Grant (Orlando, Florida) and over thirty-five years as a partner in Kane & Associates in Winter Park, Florida. He was also an accountant with Chevron Oil Company in charge of fixed asset accounting for all oil and gas properties in northern Louisiana, Mississippi, Florida and Alabama.

Gary is the managing partner of Kane & Associates. His primary responsibilities include the planning and utilization of personnel, budgeting, cash flow management, and overall firm marketing. He has been responsible for the supervision, planning, and review responsibilities for all tax preparation and planning functions within the firm. He performs the final, technical review of all audit and review engagements. Gary has lectured widely on various aspects of income tax planning, business valuation, forensic accounting and personal financial planning. He has appeared on numerous local television shows and has appeared on national cable television program broadcast on the Satellite Program Network. With his background in tax and financial planning, he has been instrumental in assisting clients in the formation, implementation and management of several real estate ventures, beginning with the planning stage through the completion and ultimate management or sale.

Mr. Kane is a member of the American and Florida Institutes of Certified Public Accountants, the National Association of Certified Valuation Analysts and is an Accredited Business Valuator, a Certified Valuation Analyst and is Certified in Financial Forensics. He is past president of the Central Florida Chapter of the International Association for Financial Planning and has served as Chairman of its Board of Directors. He has been an adjunct professor at the University of Central Florida teaching intermediate accounting and has assisted the Small Business Development Center at the University of Central Florida in lectures on business acquisitions and accounting systems for small businesses.

Gary Kane is licensed as a CPA in the State of Florida and is a member of the Collaborative Family Law Group of Central Florida. For more than twenty years, he has assisted attorneys in numerous areas, including tax planning, litigation, business valuation, expert testimony and divorce settlements. He has testified as an expert witness in Brevard, Orange, Osceola, Seminole, and Volusia Counties and in Federal Court in the Middle District of Florida.

CHAPTER 10

TIPS, TECHNIQUES AND LITTLE KNOWN SECRETS OF REAL PROPERTY OWNERSHIP

– STILL THE GREATEST "TAX SHELTER" IN THE INTERNAL REVENUE CODE

BY JOHN E. WALTERS, MBA, EA

Monday morning, just after 9:00 am, the office phone rings, it's my longtime client Joe (we'll call him Joe because that is <u>not</u> his 'real name'). He was calling with great excitement in his voice and said, "I just purchased my first investment rental property over the weekend and I need to see you right away to discuss the tax benefits of my investment."

"Okay Joe, let's meet tomorrow at 10:00 am in my office. I'll need you to bring a few things to our meeting. Please bring the big package that you received when you closed on the purchase of the new property and in particular the 'Settlement' statement that you received from your lender."

"Great!" Joe said, "tomorrow it is...see you then."

As I hung up the phone with him, I was mentally planning our meeting discussion set for the very next day and all the benefits the *Tax Code* offers to ownership of investment property.

<u>Acquiring The Property</u>
Analysis of the Settlement Statement

The Planting of the Early Tax Savings Seeds

The next day, promptly at 10 am, Joe arrived at my office, eager and excited to discuss his new investment property.

"So let's take a look at that settlement statement that you brought with you," I said, as he pulled out the lengthy statements from a large folder that the mortgage company gave him and then he handed it to me. "Joe," I said, "this document tells us the story about what you just purchased and it also contains a wealth of Tax Savings related information that will get you on the right track to all the great benefits of your investment property ownership. Are you ready to review it together?"

Joe gave me a nod of agreement. "For the first step, we will look at the settlement costs or expenses from your **Form HUD-1** *settlement statement* that you were responsible to pay for as the buyer of the property and how they relate to your present and future tax benefits," I said. From the buyer's column of the HUD-1 we reviewed the numbered rows and columns, and I related to Joe how each was either a tax benefit to him now or would be in the future – when he sold or disposed of the property.

Table 1

Form HUD-1	Settlement Costs and Expenses	Tax treatment for property Buyer
Row lines 100 - 600	Real Estate Taxes City/Town/County	Deductible beginning on the date of Sale
Row lines 100 - 600	Assessments, Condo and Assoc. Fess	Deductible beginning on the date of Sale
Row lines 700 – 704	Real Estate or Broker Commissions	Amortize over Term of the Loan
Row lines 801 – 802	Loan Origination fees or Loan discount (Points)	Amortize over Term of the Loan
Rows 803 – 811	Items payable in the connection of the loan i.e. appraisal etc.	Amortize over Term of the Loan
Rows 901	Interest	Deductible beginning on the date of Sale
Rows 902 – 905	Items required to be paid in advance such insurance policies	Deductible beginning on the date of Sale
Rows 1000 – 1008	Reserve deposits with lender	Not Deductible
Rows 1100 – 1113	Items payable in connections with the title charges	Increase basis and are capitalized
Rows 1200 – 1205	Government recording and transfer charges	Increase basis and are capitalized
Rows 1300 – 1305	Additional settlement charges i.e. surveys, pest inspections, etc.	Increase basis and are capitalized

"As you can see Joe, from Table 1, there are quite a few costs and expenses that you have paid in connection with your purchase, some we can use now on your present year tax return, and some will benefit you far into the future when you sell the property. I'm sure by this time you have realized just how important saving this document is, and that it needs to be safely maintained while you own this investment. "

"Sadly," I said, "many clients have come to me in the past when they wanted to sell their investment property and they have not kept their settlement documents from when they purchased their property, and in-turn lose many of their *valuable* benefits and ultimately end up paying more in taxes than they needed too." Upon ending our review of the Settlement statement I looked at Joe and said, "*We will not let this happen to you.*"

"Now, are you ready to take the next step and put your new investment to work for you?" Again Joe eagerly nodded in agreement, and I relayed to him that I call this the first step:

STEP I
SETTING UP THE PROPERTY FOR ACTIVE AND OPERATIONAL USE
&
GETTING IT "RIGHT THE FIRST TIME" FOR MAXIMUM BENEFIT

First, we are going to fill out a *Rental Property Setup Worksheet* using the information from your Settlement statement and in particular we'll use the following:

- Property Description, for example. 'Rental Condo'.

- Property Location, i.e. address of Investment/ Rental property.
- Date Placed in Service, i.e. date that your property is available and ready to rent.

"This last item is very important since it will help us in establishing the date to start *depreciating* your new property."

Joe looked puzzled; he asked, "What is depreciation?"

"Joe, I'm glad you asked. *Depreciation* – in its most basic definition provides a means according to the Tax Code a way to deduct or (reduce) the cost of a capital asset (in your case the investment property you bought) over a specified recovery period expressed in years. To depreciate your new investment property correctly we will need to allocate the basis (total costs paid to acquire your investment property), i.e., cost of the building and the cost of the land, which, by the way, is not depreciable. Since we are on the subject of depreciation, you'll want to know that according to the present Tax Code the life of your property building is **27.5** years."

"That's quite a long time" said Joe, "I might not even own the property for that many years."

"Well," I replied. "In that case; we may want to *supercharge* your depreciation expenses to get the most benefit right now, by using a technique to separate the "real" property from the "personal" property of your investment, which is known as *cost segregation.* By using this technique, we are not only following the rules laid out in the Tax Code but we are reducing the "tax" lives of certain "personal" property of your investment to accelerate your deductions now, reduce your current tax liabilities, and increase your present cash-flow."

"Okay, that sounds good to me, when do we start?" said Joe.

"Well," I added, "since the subject of cost segregation can be very complex...we will have to save the complex details for a later discussion. But for now, let's look at some of the other expenses and fees you have pre-paid on your settlement statement that we can use in our worksheet; property taxes paid, pre-paid homeowners insurance policies, home own- ers association fees and amortization of your loan origina- tion fees, and loan discount points."

"Are you ready to get to the next step?" I said to Joe.

"Sure" he replied.

I call this the second step:

STEP 2
YOUR FIRST YEAR IN *OPERATION* AND BEYOND
&
HARVESTING THE 'ANNUAL' TAX SAVINGS BENEFITS DURING YOUR OWNERSHIP

"For this step, we will want to once again review your Settlement statement and Table 1 information for your recurring annual expenses such as; Mortgage payments, Property taxes, Property insurance, Condo & Management fees etc. Joe, do you recall at the beginning of our discussion today, I mentioned the importance of record keeping of all the documents relating to your investment?"

"Yes, I certainly do," said Joe.

"Well now," I said. "I am going to give you a booklet that you can use to record and save all the *income* and *recurring expenses* relating to your investment. So first, let's talk about the *income* you will be receiving as rent or lease payments from your tenants which you will report each year as *'passive'* income."

"Why is it called passive income?" asked Joe.

"Well, I'm glad you asked. It's called *"passive"* income since you did not have to *earn* it as you would other types of income such as your wages from employment. You will probably also receive a *"security" deposit* payment from your tenants when they first occupy your property, but this payment <u>is not</u> considered reportable and taxable income to you if it is a *"refundable" payment* to your tenants when they complete their lease or rental agreement with you. Now, let's talk about the *recurring* expenses that you might have while your property is "in service" and occupied by your tenants."

Since the categories of expenses can be rather extensive and specific to the type of property, here is a list of typical Investment or Rental property expenses:

√	Mortgage Payments	√	Property Taxes	√	Insurance
√	Management Fees	√	Utilities	√	Landscaping
√	Wages and Salaries	√	Advertising	√	Cleaning & Maintenance
√	Commissions	√	Improvements	√	Legal & Accounting
√	Repairs	√	Supplies	√	Depreciation
√	Security	√	Auto & Travel	√	Pest Control

"Of course, you may not have "all" of these *types* of expenses and you may very well have some others not covered in this list. But we will determine what to include in this list each year that you own the property. The important thing to remember is that you will need to be a good *record keeper* so that you do not <u>lose</u> any of these valuable deductions," I said.

Tax Tip: Before we leave the subject of expenses, I do want to mention the "special" attention that the Tax Code gives to the expense types: *repair* vs. *improvement*. In general, the Tax Code states that *repairs* are expenses we can fully deduct in the year that they occur whereas an *improvement* may need to be *capitalized* and deducted (depreciated) over many years, just like your building. We will have to determine these differences each and every year when we meet to review your records.

"One final note before we move on to the third and final step in our discussion today. If after we have included all the income that you have derived from the property and deducted all the expenses for the year results in a *loss*, then this *loss* is subject to the *"passive activities"* *loss* rules," I added.

TAX TIP: The present Tax Code allows for these losses to offset other *non-passive* income from other sources (i.e. wages & salaries) within certain limitations. This can be a very valuable and beneficial way to reduce income from other sources and any tax liabilities you may have from year to year. Of course, as with any tax law there are exceptions to the *passive activity* loss rules for certain classes of entities and individuals.

"Now, let's project ourselves for a minute or two into the future to the day that you want to complete the sale or exchange of your investment property. Are you ready to see what happens then?" I said to Joe.

"Okay" he said, shaking his head.

I call this the third and final step:

STEP 3
FINAL YEAR IN OPERATION AND PROPERTY DISPOSAL
&
REAPING THE TAX SAVING BENEFITS OF AN INVESTMENT SALE

"Joe, since you and I have worked together throughout the ownership period of this property, I know that you have kept good records of all the activities with this property so now it is time to reap your rewards and let's look at the tax aspects of the property sale. We can explore the possibility of a *Like-Kind* property exchange and defer any taxes on the sale far into the future, possibly forever but this subject is just as complex as the subject of *cost segregation,* so we will leave that as a topic for a later discussion. As you will recall Joe, we had to originally set up your rental property and establish a basis for de*preciation pu*rposes and allocate some of the costs of the purchase to the building and some to the land. Now, as the property seller, you have a final sales price for your property. This is usually located on your seller's *Settlement Statement* just as when you bought the property so many years ago."

"Next we want to subtract from your sales price the "expenses" that you incurred to sell your property. When we subtract these selling expenses, we now have the "amount realized" from the property sale. But before we conclude what *"taxable"* gain or loss you may have on the sale we must calculate the "adjusted" basis in the property, and for that we will need to take a look at your original purchase *Settlement Statement* for the following items:

1. Expenses for acquisition (i.e. costs we had to capitalize)
2. List of capital improvements throughout your ownership period.

Now Joe, it's time to account for all those years of *depreciation* we took and benefitted from as the owner of the property. This will be subtracted from the "adjusted" basis as above to arrive at the property's final adjusted basis and the *"taxable"* gain or loss on the sale. One final note, if you had any "suspended" losses in the prior years of your ownership due to the *Passive Activity* loss limitations we will use them to offset any taxable gain that you may have on the sale."

As you can see, it can become quite complex to arrive at that "final" tax figure on the sale. By employing the help and advice of a Tax Professional with expert knowledge in Real Estate transactions can ensure you maximize your ownership benefits, and help you reduce any taxes on the transaction to the lowest levels possible.

When our meeting that day concluded, Joe realized that there was quite a bit more to his property investment than he once thought. With property logbook in hand, he departed the office with a commitment to "stay in touch" often regarding his new investment.

Would you like to receive the same benefits as Joe? Then feel free to contact the author of this chapter at: <u>John@ lewaltconsulting.com</u> with your questions.

ABOUT JOHN

John E. Walters, BS, MBA, EA has been a tax practitioner for 24 years and is the founder of LeWalt Consulting Groupe, LLC. His practice focuses on developing tax and financial strategies for his varied and diverse US and International clientele.

He formed this accounting and financial services firm with a single purpose in mind: *To provide his clients with the highest level of **personalized, professional** client service possible.*

John holds an MBA in Finance and Accounting from Southern Polytechnic State University and a BS in Engineering from San Diego State University. He holds the FINRA Series 7 & 66 securities licenses. He is the past President of the FSEA Sun Coast Chapter of Enrolled Agents and a Graduate Fellow of the National Tax Practice Institute.

If you would prefer to develop a relationship with a Professional Accounting and Financial services firm that **wants** to know your name, and **understand** your *unique* needs... then get to know ... **LeWalt Consulting Groupe, LLC.**

You can contact John at: john@lewaltconsulting.com with your questions.

CHAPTER 11

HOW TO STAY OUT OF TROUBLE WITH THE IRS (AND WHAT TO DO IF YOU ALREADY ARE....)

BY DARRIN MISH, ESQ.

I f you are a small business owner, then chances are you have owed the IRS taxes at some point in time. If you haven't then it's only a matter of time, unless of course you follow the suggestions in this chapter. It's really unfair because they don't teach us how to take care of our tax obligations in college, or even law school! The government just assumes that small business owners know what they're doing, or maybe something more sinister is afoot. Did you know that the IRS has over 150 penalties at it's disposal when you make a mistake in preparing, filing or paying your taxes? And that's before we even start talking about interest on top of unpaid taxes. Suffice it to say, tax liabilities owed to the IRS grow fast, and don't stop until they're paid (or you manage to avoid paying in full by filing an Offer in Compromise or filing bankruptcy).

Winston Churchill once said "Let our advance worrying become advance thinking and planning." This statement is never truer than with taxes. Since the preparation of taxes is one of American's most dreaded annual rituals, it is fair to say that we should attempt to make the best of the situation and be smart about our planning.

The best way to preplan for taxes, especially for an individual, is to make estimated tax payments. This will alleviate the burden of a large tax bill and reduce it to a quarterly payment that you can more easily manage. Since I have been practicing tax law for almost the last two decades, I have seen many clients who could have prevented their entire tax burden by making estimated tax payments. Instead, they allowed the situation to spiral out of control, and beyond their reach to resolve the matter on their own. With added penalties and interest accruing from unpaid tax debts, they have turned small liabilities over a number of years into six-figure tax burdens. The first piece of advice that I give them is START making estimated tax payments and then we will fix the outstanding balances.

Lets assume for a minute that we were talking about first aid. In the case of bleeding, one must first attend to the bleeding and stop it before remedying the wound. Failure to do so will ultimately result in the death of the person. If you already have unpaid taxes, then you are going to have to treat the making of estimated tax payments as the triage you need. If you try to negotiate a settlement, payment plan or other collection alternatives, the IRS will look at your problem and your increasing liabilities much like bleeding. If you leave this important factor in your situation unresolved, the IRS will know how to stop the bleeding ...with pressure! The reality is the past can be overcome, but you MUST STOP allowing new IRS liabilities to accrue.

In order to plug the money hole, the IRS can require an individual to make estimated tax payments. If an individual fails to do so, the IRS will impose penalties for the failure to make timely payments. Generally, taxpayers who anticipate they will owe taxes in the upcoming year should ensure that their withholdings and/or estimated tax payments will equal more than 90% of the anticipated liability. If you are unable to do so, you will discover that many of the collection alternatives discussed later in this chapter are not available to you at the negotiation table. Staying current and compliant going forward is imperative; without this commitment the IRS sees you as a continued liability and knows that there is no benefit to negotiating with you – as the problem will only be perpetuated. This is certainly not an admirable position to be in as a taxpayer, though understandably logical from the viewpoint of the IRS.

In determining your requirement with regard to estimated payments, the IRS will factor in your last year's tax return liability and current withholdings from your paycheck. For a small business, they will also use your profit and loss statement. You can determine the same information by completing a current year estimated tax form. Detailed instructions and additional information regarding estimated taxes can be found on Form 1040-ES for the current year. You can download this form and obtain up-to-date information about deadlines, exceptions and payment options at: http://www.irs.gov

Wage earners can submit a new Form W-4 to your employer, therefore adjusting your withholdings and eliminating the need to pay estimated tax payments. The Form W-4 also includes a worksheet to help you determine the correct amount of withholding that you should be deducting from each paycheck. Form W-4 can be found at: http://www.irs.gov

Any corporation that is required to make estimated tax payments will need to download the Form 1120-W to figure the required payment amounts. You can read the IRS Publication 542 for more information regarding the requirements of a corporation. This usually is not applicable if you have the most common sort of small business corporation called a Sub S corporation. Since the Sub S is a 'flow thru' entity – meaning the individual shareholders are taxed on the profits of the corporation – the Sub S typically owes no tax, and therefore has no need to make its own Estimated Tax Payments.

You have the option of paying your Estimated Tax Payments by a variety of methods. An individual can submit the payments with a payment voucher that is attached within the Form 1040 ES worksheet. You will need to mail your tax payment and form to the Internal Revenue Service address indicated on the 1040-ES form. When mailing payments, you must indicate in the memo line your social security number, tax form and year for the payment to be applied correctly. An individual may also use the EFTPS (electronic federal tax payment system). You must obtain a pin number by applying to the IRS to use this feature, but it can be a convenient way to make timely payments at your leisure.

In 2011, most companies and businesses are required to make all payments by the EFTPS system. Companies and small business who fail to meet this requirement could be subject to additional penalties. If you are wondering if Estimated Tax Payments apply to you, the IRS has a Publication 505 that is available for download from their website. The basic formula for determining if you owe estimated tax payments, before a penalty of under withholding is an issue, is to determine if you owe less than $1000 in tax or if you have paid at least 90% of your current taxes or 100% of your prior tax year's liability.

There will be individuals who cannot use the typical method of paying quarterly tax returns. If your income fluctuates drastically, the determination of estimated tax payments may be more difficult. You can use Form 2210 from the IRS to attach to your Form 1040 at the end of the year. This form will allow you to possibly determine alternative circumstances that could forgive any penalty for failure to pay your estimated tax payments.

Over the years representing thousands of taxpayers, a significant number of these clients could have easily avoided the heartache that an IRS problem brings simply by making estimated tax payments. I understand that it's easier said than done. Often times the problem was caused by pure ignorance of the obligation to make quarterly payments; thinking that they "will catch up in the future," or that it would be a better use of the funds to just pay the entire tax debt at the end of the year. All of these reasons are 'off base.' As a small business owner myself, I know how it is. There is always a better use for the money today for the business rather than paying it over to the IRS. But I have come up with a solution that works for me and has worked for many of my clients over the years.

Many years ago, when just starting my law practice, I had an IRS problem of my own. It was under $10,000, but at the time I felt it was impossible to deal with, and I had no idea how I was ever going to get out from under the debt. I was newly married and like many people in this situation, I hid it from my spouse. One day the pressure became too great, and I told my wife what was going on. She was very understanding and came up with a solution that I use to this day and have advised hundreds of clients to utilize as well. You see, most taxpayers see that the estimated payments are due quarterly, and just assume that they cannot be made more frequently. Nothing could be farther from the truth. You can make estimated payments to the IRS every day if you like. The advice goes like this. If you are a sole proprietor or if you're taking distributions from your Sub S Corporation, take 25-30% off the top when you pay yourself. Then you either segregate this money into a separate bank account to be paid to the IRS quarterly, or if you have trouble saving money, send it to the IRS on a Estimated Tax coupon as often as you like. This could be daily, weekly, monthly or whenever you pay yourself. Is this the magic bullet? No. But it keeps you in the ballpark. If you follow this regimen and only have income from the business, you should be much better off than if you didn't make any estimated tax payments at all.

However, if you do find yourself with a tax obligation, one of the most important tips, nuggets or pieces of advice is, when choosing between paying past due taxes or current taxes always pay current tax first. Let me say that again. Always pay current taxes before paying past due taxes. You must show goodwill through becoming compliant if you hope to negotiate past offences. I know that this adjustment to income can be difficult and seems almost impossible. I also know from experience that self-imposed triage is easier than when the IRS demands a remedy! Having a plan in place, even if not immediately realistic, can go a long way at the negotiation table!

There are six alternatives to collection by the IRS if you find yourself with a tax bill larger than you can afford to pay. They are:

1. Installment Agreement
2. Offer in Compromise
3. Waiting for the Collection Statute of Limitations on Collection to expire
4. Bankruptcy
5. Innocent Spouse
6. Hardship Status

#1. An **Installment Agreement** is exactly what it sounds like. It's a payment arrangement with the IRS. If you owe under $10,000 and can pay off the debt within 3 years, the IRS must grant you an installment agreement (unless you have had a prior installment agreement in preceding years). If you owe under $25,000 and full pay the liability within 5 years, they may grant you an installment agreement without requiring that you submit exhaustive financial reports of your personal and business affairs.

#2. An **Offer in Compromise** is when you are able to make a deal with the IRS. In certain situations, when the IRS determines that their best deal would be to take some money from you now rather than try to collect all the money over time, it's possible to make a deal for pennies on the dollar. This is an exhaustive process, requiring significant investigation. It works well for people with no assets and a low income. I have personally settled $99,000 debts for $1,000 but every taxpayer's situation varies. These are not simple cases and may require an attorney to help you through the process.

#3. The **Collection Statute of Limitations** for **Collection** is actually a secret that the IRS keeps from us as taxpayers. In short, the IRS has ten years from the date of the assessment of the tax to collect it. In a typical situation, if you file a tax return with a balance due, the tax is assessed at the time of filing and the IRS then has only ten years to collect. Of course, there are different situations where taxes are assessed much later than when the return is filed. One such situation is in the typical audit scenario. In this scenario, the tax return is filed and selected for audit two years later. The audit takes six months or a year and then the additional tax is assessed. This results in a practical situation where the IRS has over ten years from the date of the filing of the return but still only had ten years from the assessment of the tax.

This is usually not a great tool if the tax years in question are rather recent, but can be great if the tax debt is older. For example, if you have a balance with only 3 years remaining on the collection statute and the IRS decides to put you into an installment agreement, they can decide to give you a payment that will NOT full pay the liability during those three years. This is called a partial pay installment agreement and could result in a taxpayer paying only a fraction of the total.

#4. Most people (including bankruptcy attorneys) don't know that personal income taxes can be discharged in **bankruptcy** if the circumstances are just right. There are five factors to consider when determining whether income tax liabilities are dischargeable in bankruptcy.

1. It must have been more than three years from the due date of the return including extensions
2. The tax returns, if filed late, must have been filed for more than 2 years.
3. The tax must have been assessed for more than 240 days.
4. The tax return must have been non-fraudulent.
5. Taxpayer must not have been guilty of willful attempt to evade or defeat the tax.

This is highly technical subject matter here. It is advisable that you consult an attorney very familiar with this subject matter. A tiny mistake could result in the filing of a bankruptcy that fails to discharge your tax obligation. This could be catastrophic and is to be avoided at all costs.

#5. **Innocent Spouse** is a remedy used by taxpayers who assert that the tax obligation is or should be the obligation of their former spouse and not their own. It is highly technical, and is a poorly written law in my opinion. If you used to be married, and believe that your former spouse should be held responsible for the tax debt, it's worth looking into.

#6. Lastly, we have **hardship status.** If the IRS determines that you have no ability to pay your tax debt, they may place you in hardship status (also known as *currently not collectible*). During this time, penalties and interest do continue to accrue, but the statute of limitations for collection and the time limitations for bankruptcy also continue to run. This can be used to better situate yourself in order to get the best resolution possible, without the requirement to make monthly payments.

In conclusion, IRS problems can be very tough to resolve. The best course of action is to avoid them by making estimated tax payments. If it's too late to avoid a tax bill, get current by making estimated tax payments if necessary and then consider the six collection alternatives discussed above. Typically, these problems can be resolved without a total disruption of your personal and financial life.

ABOUT DARRIN

Darrin Mish, Esq. graduated from Golden Gate University, in San Francisco, California in 1993 with a Doctor of Jurisprudence. He was admitted to the Florida Bar in that same year and the Bar of the State of Colorado in 2002. He has earned an AV rating from Martindale-Hubbell, the country's most popular attorney rating service. An AV rating signifies an attorney that has "achieved the highest levels of professional skill and integrity." The AV rating is based upon peer reviews by other members of the Bar and the judiciary. Lawyers and judges in the larger community have been polled by Martindale-Hubbell and, based upon their submissions, the company has granted him the highest available rating for his legal skills, as well as for honesty and integrity. He has been honored to have his name placed in Martindale-Hubbell's Bar Register of Preeminent Lawyers as well.

This means that you, the client, receive aggressive representation from a young, energetic, honest, yet experienced attorney. Mr. Mish is permitted to practice before the United States Supreme Court; all courts of the State of Florida; the State of Colorado; the United States District Court, Middle District of Florida; United States Court of Appeals, 11th Circuit; United States Tax Court; United States Court of Federal Claims; the United States Court of Appeals, Federal Circuit; United States Court of Appeals, District of Columbia Circuit; and the United States District Court, Northern District of Florida. He has taken the extra steps to be admitted before all of these courts because he is committed to helping you with your IRS problems, including appeals.

In 2002, Mr. Mish was awarded "Practitioner of the Year" by the American Society of IRS Problem Solvers. He is a member of the Tax Freedom Institute, the American Bar Association, the National Association of Tax Professionals, the National Association of Criminal Defense Lawyers, the Florida Association of Criminal Defense Lawyers, and the Hillsborough County Bar Association. These memberships help him stay current with the law and enable him to protect your rights.